The Mountain Cafe Cookbook

A Kiwi in the Cairngorms

First published in the UK in 2017 by

Kitchen Press Ltd
1 Windsor Place
Dundee
DD2 1BG

Recipes © Kirsten Gilmour 2017
Illustrations © Elizabeth Pirie 2017
Photographs © Paul Masson 2017 and © Kirsten Gilmour 2017
Design © Andrew Forteath 2017

ISBN 978-0-9570373-8-0

A catalogue record for this book is available
from the British Library

Printed in Scotland by Bell and Bain Ltd

The Mountain Cafe Cookbook

A Kiwi in the Cairngorms

Kirsten Gilmour

KITCHEN PRESS

Introduction

My passion for food started from the minute I could put it in my mouth. I was never going to be a fussy child or an unhealthy one. My mother was 18 when I was born and we were lucky enough to start the first part of our life together living on my grandparents' farm in Temuka, South Island, New Zealand. I know everyone says his or her grandparents are the best, but mine really were! They taught me everything about love and respect and about sitting and enjoying food as a family, the European way.

Nana and Granddad's six acre farm had a huge vegetable patch and an orchard; the glasshouses bulged with tomatoes, cucumbers, gherkins and peppers; they raised sheep, pigs, geese, ducks, chickens, even the occasional cow. We lived like lords on delicious home-killed meat.

At a young age I found solace in food and cooking. I loved helping Nana and Granddad make their green tomato pickle or scraping new potatoes with Granddad at the old barbecue table in the garden. Flipping pikelets and sitting down to a huge plate with raspberry jam and whipped cream was heavenly.

My grandparents didn't have massive amounts of money, but occasionally they would take me to George's, a Swiss German-style restaurant in nearby Timaru. George's was always a really special treat. I was fascinated with the big steamy coffee machine and the frothy stuff that came out of it. Nana would drink this amazing frothy coffee and Granddad would speak in a strange language with George; it felt like another world. The highlight of these outings was when George would take me into the bustling kitchen, full of chefs working away and shiny copper pans and salamis hanging from the ceiling. The smells of sauces on the gas burner were divine. At the age of five I had already found my calling in life.

School was a waste of time for me; I hated it. But when I ended up doing my chef exams at Aoraki Polytechnic, everything changed. The tutors were an awesome bunch, but one in particular turned my life around. Lindsay Bennett was everything I dreamt of being in a chef. He was smart, hardworking, talented beyond belief and his knowledge was mind blowing. The best thing about Lindsay was that he inspired me and made me realise there was a whole world out there, that I would never stop learning about food. I still visit him at his restaurant in Timaru whenever I am home to eat his food and hear his amazing tales. Our carrot cake recipe comes from him and I can never share it, as it took me two years of moaning at him to get it.

When I was 20, I was part of the polytechnic culinary team put forward for the New Zealand Culinary Fare. It was a big deal, and we won gold. That prize helped me scrape together enough cash for a one-way ticket to the UK – and here the adventure really began. For the next few years I worked my ass off, in good jobs and bad. I experienced everything from Michelin-starred hotels to London fine dining and ended up in Annie O'Carroll's great fusion restaurant, Luca. I loved it. In my first week,

Annie had me smashing octopus tentacles against the outside kitchen wall, just like she had done on the rocks in Tunisia. She taught me a huge amount about flavour combinations and techniques, and also how to make a damn good salad.

It was a crazy couple of years, so when she sold the restaurant, I decided it was time to move on from London and go travelling. I gave up my room in the flat, loaded my backpack, knives and whites, bought a train ticket and headed north. I ate my way around England and Scotland, and eventually found myself in Aviemore looking for a weekend of skiing. If someone had told me then that in three years' time I would be settled here, married to a Scotsman and about to take over the Mountain Cafe, I would have laughed in their face.

When I arrived in Aviemore, I went straight to an outdoor shop to hire some skis. I was served by the manager, who mentioned he was short-staffed and was looking for a shop assistant. The perks were a free ski pass, free ski hire and a great bunch of guys to work with. It was 2001 and the best ski season to hit Cairngorm in a good few years. I wasn't even thinking about work, but the idea of skiing and drinking lots of beer while earning some money seemed pretty inviting.

It was nice to have a break from cooking and working day and night. I learnt to rock climb, mountain bike and hill walk, hobbies that I had never had time for before. I made some incredible friends. We climbed hills, bivvied out and had epic adventures – it was the most amazing, carefree six months,

during which I met Al who I married another six months later in New Zealand.

We came back to Scotland and suddenly we were buying a house, Al was setting up an outdoor activity company and I was getting the itch to cook again, so I catered for his groups and was their number one slave. When we didn't have trips running, I worked in Cairngorm Mountain Sports to get a bit of pocket money and cheap kit. This was when I first experienced the Mountain Cafe, which was upstairs from the shop. Every day folks would come down and moan about how terrible the food was and how unfriendly the service was. And every day I would say to my work mates, 'That place is a waste! It needs some Kiwiana injected into it!' My blethering paid off. I received a text saying that the cafe was coming up for rent and one of the guys from work had told the landlord all about my rants and dreams. I met the landlord the next day and he offered it to me, so I made a panicked phone call to my parents-in-law to ask for a loan and two weeks later I was holding the keys to the Mountain Cafe.

The cafe came with rickety tables and chairs, peach tartan curtains, horrific lighting, a griddle (which went on fire), a knackered oven (which blew up), a fridge, a freezer (both household) and a tired old dishwasher that was the size of a glass washer. I had borrowed £9k off my parents-in-law and that had to cover crockery, cutlery, glassware, the first month's rent, rates, wages, first suppliers' payments and the rental on a coffee machine. I stripped everything out of our kitchen at home; we didn't have a pot or pan left. My mother-in-law donated a cake mixer and mini deep-fat fryer. We raided, borrowed and Ikea-shopped, and friends scrubbed, painted, peeled, stirred, sweated, chopped and washed dishes. The support was immense. I was 26, thinking I'd have a nice wee cafe, a handful of staff, maybe 50 covers a day, with evenings free to bike and have adventures. I was totally oblivious to the monster it was about to become.

We really hit the ground running. What do I remember the most from the cafe's early days? Hmmm. Not having a day off for four months, working at least 14 hours a day, trying to do kitchen and front of the house myself, sleeping on the floor in the storeroom because I was too tired to drive home, having friends help me bake till 1am in the morning... Being determined that I was not going to buy cakes in, that I would make everything possible from scratch using local foods... Getting systems in place, finding a strong crew and keeping everything as consistent as possible. And then there were the disasters like emptying the deep fat fryer all over the floor after a 13-hour day, or the time I set fire to the wall grill which then spread to the extraction system – we had to call the fire brigade out two hours before a function began – and so the list continued....

It was a huge learning curve. The first year we were open, we made a massive financial loss, so much so I almost lost the place. But with a lot of hard work, good advice, sleepless nights, Kiwi Sauvignon Blanc, determination and a passion that somehow remained with me throughout the whole journey, we finally got to the place that is now the MC Aviemore.

In this book I wanted to give folks an insight into how the Mountain Cafe came into being, share our secrets, make you laugh and inspire you to get creative in the kitchen.

I really hope it does just that....

Have Confidence In Yourself

A day doesn't go by at the café when we aren't asked for recipes. We get e-mails begging us for our chowder recipe, our chocolate cake or even asking how we put that fancy swirl on top of the coffees. I love it when customers and MC friends take time out to contact us, and that their little taste of the café has inspired them to recreate our dishes and cook for friends and family.

Cooking should be enjoyed and shared; it doesn't need to be a chore or a hidden fear. So take a deep breath, reach for a glass of your favourite wine or beer, turn some music on, shove on an apron, warm up the oven and away you go. Don't over-think everything, don't tell yourself you can't get timings right, that you don't have the correct pan or that you couldn't get the exact ingredient you wanted.

Cooking is all about experimenting, tasting, enjoying, socialising and having a laugh.

For the less-experienced cooks, chefs and homemakers who pick up this book, I want to help you to panic less, to enjoy the process and to feel more at home in your kitchen. I really want you to be relaxed and be able to love cooking. Some of my best food memories involve sitting around a table with friends and family. Just remember your friends are coming to dinner at your house because of your company.

Good food doesn't mean slaving over a hot stove for three hours. Making a sexy antipasti or simple salad is, in my eyes, more of a skill than chaining yourself to the oven for the day. It's sociable fun, healthy and delicious. Simple, fresh and fuss-free is the way forward. Let your artistic side come out and play!

So, here are some tips from the café to help you: plan ahead, read recipes before you start cooking, write a shopping list so you have all your ingredients at hand. Please, use our recipes and recreate our dishes, but don't be scared to add ingredients or take them out where it suits you. I am forever changing recipes and dishes. Follow your own instincts. Taste, smell and feel everything and you are one step closer to being a fantastic cook.

Basics

OLIVE OIL
A good extra virgin olive oil is pretty expensive, so for cooking I use a lower grade, cheaper olive oil and keep my fancy expensive oil for salad dressings and for finishing and garnishing prepared foods. Vegetable oil is fine for cooking at home if you don't have olive oil. Store in a pantry or somewhere out of direct sunlight.

STOCKS

In our soup section you will come across three recipes for homemade stocks. I can't rave more about homemade stock – it's a great thrifty way to get rid of leftover bones and vegetables, and adds a whole heap of flavour to your soups and stews. Using homemade stocks also massively reduces the amount of salt going into your food and you'll never have to worry about it containing wheat or gluten. You can tub up your stock, cool it down and freeze until you need it. In all the recipes, we have included measurements for using stock cubes as well as we totally get that not everyone wants to make stock or maybe you just don't have the ingredients to make them at the time.

FRESH HERBS

Lots of our recipes use big handfuls of fresh herbs. We have a huge tray of fresh herbs delivered every day to the café as I can't cook without them and I hope these recipes will inspire you to get some herb pots and have them on hand at all times. It will change your cooking and life for the better, I promise!

If you don't grow your own herbs, you can buy them, chop them up, put them in wee tubs and keep in the freezer. They will not look as appealing, but you will still get the amazing flavours. Dried herbs are handy, but the downside is they lose flavour over time and need to be used fairly quickly.

Always wash your herbs (and your spinach, leeks, etc) before you use them so you don't get a mouthful of soil.

SALT AND PEPPER

The word used most in this book is 'season'. It simply means add salt and pepper to the dish you are making. We season everything we cook and make at the café. The only advice I can give is taste often and season a little at a time as you go: it's all about tasting and tweaking to bring out the flavour in your food.

BUTTER AND CREAM

Don't scrimp on the butter and cream ever! As a chef butter and cream are the porn stars of the kitchen. I know they're full of fat, but they taste so damn good and they are a natural food – I detest margarine and pretend butter. If you want sexy food, go all the way with double cream and salted butter. I am not saying chuck it in everything, but when you are making mash, scrambled eggs, fish chowder and porridge it makes all the difference. When a recipe says butter, assume it's salted unless stated otherwise.

EGGS

We always use large, free-range eggs at room temperature – it's better for baking and safer when cracking into a hot pan of oil.

NUTS AND SEEDS

We toast all the nuts and seeds in our salads, potato rosti and slices: it brings out the natural oils and increases the flavours. Spread them on a baking sheet and toast for six minutes in a preheated oven at 180°C (160°C fan). You can also flash them in a dry pan over a medium heat for a few minutes; you don't want to brown them.

Equipment

KNIVES

I can't bang on enough about how important it is to have a good knife that you keep sharp. Get yourself a knife sharpener and make sure you use it: knives scare people and often people think it's safer for the knife to be blunt. It's not! The more blunt the knife is, the more pressure you will put on it when chopping and that's when you will cut yourself really badly. Don't put knives in the dishwasher; it ruins the handle and makes them blunt quicker.

CHOPPING BOARD

Get a decent board that is really solid. I use a big wooden one at home and I love it. Put a wet J cloth underneath the board to stop it moving around while you are chopping.

The World of Ovens

ELECTRIC

Most ovens have two electric coils, one at the top and one on the bottom, with the oven tending to be hotter at the top, so for baking a cake you are best to put the tin nearer the bottom of the oven. If you have a fan oven your food will cook quicker than in a standard electric oven: you would normally drop the cooking temperature by 20°C. Our recipes have temperatures for both ovens.

GAS

Gas ovens are notorious for having hot spots – you can avoid these by rotating your trays, tins or dishes every so often. There is no fan to even out the heat, so you need to plan where you are going to put your foods. If you are baking a cake, put it in the middle or higher in the oven to prevent the bottom burning. If you want nice crispy roast spuds, put them lower in the oven, where the main heat is coming from.

AGA/RAYBURNS

As well as an electric oven I have a Rayburn at home and it used to scare the hell out of me for baking. I bought an internal thermometer so I could adjust the dial until it was at the correct temperature. Once you're sure about the temperature, they are amazing for providing a consistent heat that doesn't seem to fluctuate much: the heat comes from the sides and the bottom of the oven, so you can open the oven door without worrying about cakes flopping, as the built-up heat remains in the oven.

Bread is awesome cooked in a Rayburn and I cook pizzas and focaccia straight onto the bottom of the hot part of the oven, giving a crispy base and a quick rise.

DE-CLUTTER

My number one piece of advice for cooking at home is to get rid of all the clutter you don't use from your worktops. It will improve your workflow and reduce your stress. Trying to prepare food while moving ornaments and pieces of kit you haven't used in months is a pain in the bum. I always keep my worktops as clear as possible. All the appliances and equipment I don't use often go in cupboards or on top of the fridge, stored away until needed.

My other top tip is clean as you go; wash your dishes as you go, keep tidying as you go and by the time you sit down most of the hard work is done and you can enjoy your meal without that horrible feeling of, 'Uh oh, I have a huge mess to clean up after this!'

Food for Folks with Dietary Requirements

A good few years ago, I went on a biking holiday with a girlfriend who had a gluten and wheat allergy. We headed off on our epic trip and it was my first exposure to what it's like to live with coeliac disease. It turned into a trip of education for me. At a lot of places we stopped to eat at, my friend would be told that the food was safe for her and free from wheat and gluten. I have never seen someone throw up so much on one trip; it was awful. Trying to get enough food into her to fuel her for these huge days on the bikes was a nightmare, so we quickly decided to make our own food in the evenings in our tent. At the end of the holiday we went out for a celebratory meal in a restaurant that looked like a place we could trust. But guess what, it wasn't and she spent the last night of the trip in the ferry bathroom.

When I took on the café, this was on my mind. I would do everything I could to make it a safe place for everyone to eat – somewhere people could really trust. Sometimes we make a mistake, but we do everything possible to avoid it: we have separate gluten free fryers, toasters, chopping boards, tongs and knives and we are really careful not to cross-contaminate.

We hose out our ovens every morning, and our dietary cakes are all made first thing, before flour starts floating about the kitchen. It's really satisfying to see people, especially kids, tucking into food that is safe and enjoyable for them, knowing how hard it is for them to find good places to eat.

This ethos runs through the book too, so we've flagged up all the recipes with the following symbols to make it easier for you to use:

 GLUTEN FREE   VEGAN   EGG FREE

 WHEAT FREE   DAIRY FREE

You can also tweak a lot of the recipes to make them suitable for restricted diets – check the recipes for suggestions.

Breakfast

My first experience of brioche was in Paris on my thirtieth birthday. On the search for a birthday treat I came out of a patisserie with a huge buttery, sexy brioche. It was so good I think I ate one every day for the rest of the trip. I love this loaf as it's a great sharing breakfast treat – it works amazingly well with sweetened cream cheese and rhubarb compote.

· Brioche does take time. You will need to get started the day before you want to eat it – the dough enriches in the fridge for 12 hours before proving and baking. It may feel like a labour of love but it is sooooo sexy!

· We make this recipe in a cake mixer with a dough hook, but you could use an electric hand-held mixer with dough hooks attached. Making by hand is also fine; you might have some serious guns once you've finished though.

· This freezes well wrapped in clingfilm. Just make sure you unwrap it and defrost on a cooling rack to stop the loaf going soggy.

Brioche

Serves 4–6, depending how greedy you feel

---

6 large eggs
50ml full fat milk
450g plain flour
8g yeast
90g caster sugar
1 teaspoon salt
270g salted butter, melted
30g desiccated coconut
30g flaked coconut
100g dark chocolate chips

23 x 13cm loaf tin

Put your eggs, milk, flour, yeast, sugar and salt into your mixing bowl. Either put your dough hook onto the mixer and start mixing or use your hands (and guns) to make a very sticky but smooth and evenly mixed dough. If you're using your hands you'll need to lightly flour a clean work surface and knead the dough for around ten minutes until smooth. Start adding the melted butter, bit by bit, until it's fully incorporated and you have sloppy, elastic and messy-looking dough. If you're doing this by hand you'll need to put the dough back into a large mixing bowl before adding the butter slowly and kneading it in. You need to make sure you get the butter evenly mixed through, and the resulting dough will be very sticky and wet.

Add the coconut and the chocolate chips and mix in thoroughly. Take a large plastic mixing bowl and spray with a little vegetable oil to stop the dough from sticking. Place the dough into the greased bowl, cover with clingfilm and leave at room temperature for an hour. Put it in the fridge for another 12 hours, then in the morning remove the bowl of dough and leave out on the bench for one more hour to get back to room temperature.

Grease and flour your loaf tin. Lightly flour a clean work surface and tip the dough onto it. Split it into three even pieces and shape each piece into a smooth ball. Place the balls into the loaf tin with the smoothest side facing up. Leave to prove for one hour covered with a clean tea towel. Then bake in a preheated oven at 170°C (150°C fan) for about 1 hour 15 minutes or until a skewer comes out clean. Tip the loaf straight out of the tin onto a rack so it doesn't go soggy – but make sure you chop a chunk off to eat while it's still hot!

I am an absolute sucker for eggy bread; I can't go past it on any menu. My most memorable was in San Francisco: the city is French toast heaven with its unbelievable artisan breads and winning toppings.

· We use chunky ciabatta bread and soak it overnight, meaning that it's eggy and moist right to the middle. Depending on the how thick your bread is, you can keep a tub in the fridge for up to three days.

· If the bread is cut too thin it will fall apart and dissolve into the egg mix.

French Toast

Serves 4

8 large eggs
600ml double cream
4 teaspoons cinnamon
4 teaspoons nutmeg
8 slices ciabatta bread, at least
  3cm thick
1 tablespoon vegetable oil

Whisk together the eggs, cream and spices. Give it a really good beat until the mix is pale and smooth then tip into a large tub or bowl. Take your slices of bread, place them in the tub and give each piece a light squeeze in the egg mix to make sure it is fully coated – this will also help stop them all sticking together. Leave in the fridge to soak for at least an hour, preferably overnight.

Preheat your oven to 180°C (160°C fan). When it's time to cook, heat the oil in a heavy-bottomed frying pan over a medium heat. Working in batches, add as many pieces of the egg-soaked bread as you can comfortably fit and cook on both sides until golden brown. Fire the pan straight into the oven or put the bread on a baking tray then bake until cooked in the middle but still moist (five to ten minutes). I like it when there is still a tiny bit of gooeyness.

You can top with whatever you like, but here are some ideas from the café:

· Fresh fruit salad
· Crispy bacon
· Grilled banana with cinnamon sugar
· Blueberry compote (page 43)
· Fresh berries
· Stewed raspberries (page 40)
· Greek-style natural yogurt
· The obvious one is maple syrup. But why not try out my lime and mint syrup recipe (page 44) for a summer zing?

This was originally my nana's pikelet recipe, which I think she adapted from a copy of her mother's *Edmonds Cookery Book*. I loved making these with her. She would stand and supervise while I stood on a chair flipping away. My granddad and I would then sit at the kitchen table stuffing in hot pikelets with lashings of whipped cream and raspberry jam. Poor Nana would never sit with us – she was too busy cleaning up my mess! I guess that's where I get my clean-freakishness from now.

· Place a damp cloth under the mixing bowl while you are whisking – the bowl won't run away on you so you won't have to hold it so tight.

· The batter can be made the night before and kept in the fridge.

· When you add the butter to the pan it should not burn or go brown; if it does, the pan is too hot.

· Never ever, ever make these in advance and try to reheat them. Nana will frown down upon you – it is a criminal offence not to eat them straight from the pan.

Pancakes

Serves 4

3 large eggs
145g caster sugar
300ml full fat milk
400g plain flour
4 teaspoons baking powder
10g salted butter

Break the eggs into a large mixing bowl and add the sugar. Using a whisk, beat the absolute hell out of them (Nana's words would be, 'give them billio Kj!'). You want to beat until the mix is pale, light and fluffy – you could use an electric mixer if you have one. Now add the milk, flour and baking powder and whisk vigorously until you have a smooth batter.

Heat a heavy-bottomed non-stick frying pan till hot over a medium heat. Carefully drop half the butter into the pan and rub it around using a little kitchen paper, being careful not to burn yourself. Now the pan is greased and at temperature, drop in a small spoon of batter to make a test pancake. The first pancake is usually not great, but as the pan gets to an even heat they will cook to a lovely golden brown.

If the pan is hot enough, pour large spoonfuls of batter into the pan and cook until the underside is golden and you start to see bubbles forming on the top of the pancake. Then it's time to flip them and cook for another minute or so on the other side.

If the pancakes start to stick, re-grease the pan with the remaining butter using the method above.

Serve hot straight from the pan and maybe give them a try with our cardamom oranges (page 36).

I was inspired to do this as a breakfast dish instead of an afternoon tea loaf after a trip to New Zealand where banana bread was all the rage. It is amazing buttered, but it is also outrageous with caramel sauce (page 46), fresh banana and stewed raspberries for brunch.

· This recipe can only be made in a food processor or a blender. I've tried making it by hand and in a cake mixer, and sadly you just don't get the same result.

· Make sure you soak the sultanas – preferably overnight at room temperature, or as long as you possibly can – until they are soft and pump.

· The riper the bananas, the better for flavour and moisture.

· Dusting the sultanas in a bit of flour stops them sinking to the bottom of the tin. This is a great thing to do for any cakes using soaked dried fruit; it means the fruit will be even throughout your baking.

Banana Bread

Serves 4–6

100g sultanas

1 Earl Grey tea bag

3 large, ripe bananas

50g salted butter

125g caster sugar

2 eggs

2 teaspoons vanilla extract

180g + 2 tablespoons
   self-raising flour

2 teaspoons bicarbonate
   of soda

23 x 13cm loaf tin

The night before you're going to make your banana bread, place the sultanas and the teabag in a small bowl and cover with about 300ml boiling water. Leave to soak at room temperature overnight.

The next day, preheat your oven to 170°C (150°C fan). Grease and flour the loaf tin. In a food processor, purée the bananas, butter, sugar, eggs and vanilla extract until you have a smooth liquid mixture. Now add 180g self-raising flour and the bicarb and blend again until you have a smooth runny batter. Scrape out into a mixing bowl. Drain the sultanas and discard the teabag. Toss the sultanas with the remaining two tablespoons of flour until they are all completely covered, then fold them through the banana batter.

Scrape the batter into the prepared loaf tin. Bake for about 50 minutes until a skewer comes out clean, then immediately turn the loaf out of its tin onto a cooling rack. Slice it up with a sharp bread knife while it's still warm.

Granolas

Granola makes me think of the start of summer and days off, when I love to have breakfast in the garden or on the deck: fresh fruit, yogurt and drizzles of honey followed by an outdoorsy adventure fuelled by healthy goodness. Making your own is super quick and simple, and these recipes contain much less sugar than shop-bought varieties and are salt free. Pop the granola in an airtight jar and it lasts for weeks.

· I always use maple syrup in my granola recipes; it is less heavy and sticky than honey and adds sweetness and a light nutty flavour.

· For gluten free granola, just use gluten free oats.

Nutty Seed and Sultana Granola

Serves 8

Not only is this a lovely breakfast cereal but it's also great added to a crumble topping or sprinkled on ice cream.

250g oats
65g flaked almonds
65g sunflower seeds
65g pumpkin seeds
75g sultanas
65g hazelnuts
65g pistachios
2½ tablespoons
  golden caster sugar
5 teaspoons ground cinnamon
200ml maple syrup
125ml vegetable oil

Preheat your oven to 170°C (150°C fan). Place the oats, flaked almonds, sunflower seeds, pumpkin seeds, sultanas, hazelnuts, pistachios, sugar and cinnamon into a mixing bowl and mix through with your hands. Whisk the maple syrup and vegetable oil together in a small bowl and pour over the dry ingredients. Mix until everything is coated in the oily syrup. Spread in an even layer on a large baking tray and bake for 15 minutes. Take out of the oven and mix the granola with a fork, breaking up any large clumps. Bake for a further 10 minutes, then turn it over with the fork again. Leave to cool and put in an airtight jar to store.

Cranberry, Coconut and Vanilla Granola

Serves 8

This is delicious with Greek-style yogurt, fresh fruits and a cheeky drizzle of maple syrup.

250g jumbo oats
50g pumpkin seeds
50g sunflower seeds
25g linseeds
25g sesame seeds
30g flaked almonds
1 vanilla pod
80ml vegetable oil
100ml maple syrup
70g dried cranberries
25g flaked coconut
10g freeze-dried berries
  (optional)

Preheat your oven to 170°C (150°C fan). Place the oats, seeds and flaked almonds into a bowl and mix through with your hands. Using a sharp knife, cut the vanilla pod in half lengthways and scrape the pulp out into a small bowl. Add the vegetable oil and the maple syrup and whisk together until combined. Pour over the dry ingredients then stir and fold until everything is fully coated in the oily syrup. Spread the mix in an even layer on a large baking tray and bake for 15 minutes. Remove from the oven and mix through the granola with a fork, breaking up any clumps. Bake for a further 20 minutes, then as soon as you take it out of the oven, mix with a fork again. Add the cranberries, flaked coconut and freeze-dried berries while the granola is still warm and stir through with your fork. Leave to cool and put in an airtight jar to store.

What? No salt AND you put double cream in it?! Yep, sorry to all you porridge purists out there... But this actually tastes yummy and isn't a chore to eat. If you want to put a spring in your step for the rest of the day this is the breakfast you need!

- You can make this gluten free by using gluten free oats.

- Make this vegan by replacing the cream with soya or almond milk.

- Good porridge takes time, so don't rush it – you need to let the oats slowly absorb the liquid.

- Keep stirring so your porridge doesn't stick to the pan or scald.

Porridge

Serves 1

65g good quality rolled oats
280ml water
125ml double cream

Place all the ingredients into a small thick-bottomed pan and bring to the boil on a high heat, stirring all the time. Reduce the heat to low and let it simmer gently, still stirring often, until the liquid is reduced and you have lovely thick creamy porridge. The whole process should take about ten minutes.

Now fire on your favourite toppings and you are set for the day. Some of our favourites are:

- Whisky and marmalade
- Vanilla apples (page 41) with pecans and maple syrup
- Raspberries and sliced bananas
- Good old brown sugar
- Blueberries and a bit of orange zest
- Peaches with blackberries

My first experience of scrambled eggs of the non-rubbery sort was being introduced to rumbled eggs by the legend that is Lindsay Bennett. These delicious soft-but-firm, perfectly cooked bad boys had me hooked on the art of cooking awesome scrambled egg from that moment on. If I look grumpy on service it is probably because someone has asked me to cook well-done eggs…

Grumpy rules for perfect eggs:

· Rule number one… Never ever replace the cream with milk. It must be double cream, so leave your conscience at the kitchen door!

· Always whisk the eggs and cream together really well. There should be no streaks of whites – the mix should be an even consistency and a lovely golden colour.

· Always use a non-stick pan.

· If the butter in the pan goes brown at all, start again! Don't add the eggs to this pan or they will be greasy and burnt-tasting. You want the butter to be melted and just starting to sizzle.

· Don't stand and constantly stir the eggs while cooking – they should be occasionally folded away from the sides of the pan. If you over-stir they will be watery and are more likely to split.

Scrambled Eggs

Serves 1

2 large eggs
80ml double cream
1 tablespoon parsley,
  finely chopped
10g salted butter
pinch of salt
cracked black pepper

Place the eggs, cream and parsley into a mixing bowl with a pinch of salt and some black pepper. Whisk until smooth and evenly beaten. If you are having toast, fire it in the toaster now. Heat a non-stick saucepan with the butter on a medium to high heat (we use gas so we heat the pan on full and then turn it to low once the eggs are in the pan). Once the butter is melted, jiggle the pan to evenly coat the bottom – remember, no colour in the butter! – then pour in the eggs and turn the heat down to medium. Don't be tempted to start stirring straight away: give it 20 seconds and let the eggs start to cook a little around the edges of the pan without browning at all. Now take a dessert spoon and gently fold the eggs in from the side of the pan.

Keep doing this until the eggs have started to set into curds – this will take about a minute for one serving of eggs. My golden rule is to remove them when you think they are still a little underdone then set them aside while you butter your toast. By the time you come back to them, they should be perfect.

Enjoy the world of the egg snob!

I ate my first rosti on my first ever European skiing holiday to Zermatt. I am not sure what excited me more, the sexy potato dishes with warm ham and grilled eggs or just the excitement of skiing below the Matterhorn each day.

· Make your seed mix in advance and keep a jar in the pantry – it's great on salads or sprinkled over poached eggs.

· Fire in a pinch of dried chilli flakes for a wee kick.

· You can reuse the frying oil: just sieve it afterward and put it to the side for next time you cook.

· Once cooked, the rosti will keep for three days in the fridge – reheat in a dry pan, the oven or in the microwave.

Courgette, Chive and Seed Rosti

Serves 4

---

1 teaspoon sesame seeds

1 teaspoon poppy seeds

1 teaspoon linseeds

2 teaspoons sunflower seeds

2 teaspoons pumpkin seeds

½ teaspoon fennel seeds

1 medium courgette, grated

4 spring onions, finely chopped

6 chives, finely chopped

600g Maris Piper potatoes,
  peeled

3 teaspoons sea salt

1 teaspoon cracked
  black pepper

300ml olive oil for
  shallow frying

Toast all your seeds in a dry pan over a medium heat for three to four minutes until they are just starting to brown. Set aside to cool.

In a large bowl place your grated courgette, spring onion, chives and the cooled toasted seeds. Grate your potato into the same bowl, including the starchy juice that comes out of them. Add the sea salt and cracked black pepper, then use your hands to mix really well.

On a chopping board or plate split the mix into eight even piles, then squeeze and shape each one between your palms to make eight small thickish pancakes. You need to squeeze really firmly to get all the juices out – do it over the sink. Leave the rosti to sit for a few minutes. While they are resting, put the olive oil in large heavy-bottomed pan and turn onto a high heat. Go back to your rosti and again give each one a firm squeeze and a final shape, making sure they are nice and tightly bound so they won't fall apart in the pan.

To check your oil is ready, drop a couple of slithers of potato into the pan – if the oil bubbles, it's ready.

Slide four of the rosti gently into the hot oil and cook for three to four minutes on each side until golden brown. Place onto a wire rack to drain and keep in a warm oven while you cook the remaining four. Serve as part of an enormous breakfast with slow roasted tomatoes (page 35), grilled field mushrooms, sautéed spinach, poached eggs and hollandaise sauce (page 277).

Annie O'Carroll taught me many awesome things in her tiny Surbiton restaurant Luca, and slow-roasting was one of them. I loved her slow roasted tomatoes; we put them in breads, salads and with mezze-style starters. You can use them in anything you want; my personal favourite is with poached eggs, asparagus and grilled chorizo.

· Never try and rush the roasting by upping the oven temperature: they will either stew and go soggy or dry out and burn.

· You can use any other herbs if you have your own favourites.

· If you have any jars of sun-dried tomatoes or peppers marinated in oil in the fridge, use that oil instead of the olive oil for an extra flavour hit.

Slow Roasted Tomatoes

Serves 4

---

8 large, ripe vine tomatoes

1 tablespoon olive oil

4 sprigs rosemary,
  stalks removed,
  leaves finely chopped

6 sprigs thyme,
  stalks removed,
  leaves finely chopped

2 teaspoons caster sugar

1 teaspoon sea salt

1 teaspoon cracked
  black pepper

Preheat the oven to 120°C (100°C fan) and line a large baking tray with greaseproof paper. Wash your tomatoes, remove the stalks and the eye and then cut them all in half. Arrange the tomato halves on the tray, cut side facing up. Drizzle with the olive oil, and sprinkle over the chopped rosemary and thyme, sugar, salt and black pepper. Cook for two hours until the tomatoes have wrinkled and lost about half of their bulk, but are still juicy-looking. Serve straight away or leave to cool on the tray and pop into the fridge until needed.

When I'm making these at home, I love to grill the oranges on the barbecue plate for extra flavour. They make a belter of a winter brunch with pancakes and mascarpone cheese – instead of maple syrup, drizzle the cardamom syrup over the pancakes just before you eat them.

- Use the end of a rolling pin to lightly bruise the cardamom pods before adding them to the syrup – this will help release the flavour.

- For the best flavour leave these at room temperature for at least two hours before serving. The oranges will keep for up to six days in the fridge, though you might want to take the cardamom pods out of the syrup after a day or two.

Cardamom Oranges

Serves 4

110g sugar
125ml water
6 cardamom pods, bruised
4 oranges

Bring the sugar, water and cardamom pods to the boil in a saucepan and simmer until the sugar is fully dissolved. Remove from the heat and pour the syrup into a bowl. Using a sharp knife, remove the skin from the oranges and discard. Slice the oranges into thick rounds. Put a dry non-stick frying pan on a medium heat and gently cook the orange slices until lightly browned on both sides. Put them in the syrup and gently turn over so they are fully coated. Leave the oranges to cool and keep covered in the fridge until you're ready to enjoy them.

Sometimes keeping a fruit bowl of fresh fruits is impossible: they are either not ripe, all ripe at the same time, or you're rushed in the morning and don't have time to prepare them. This recipe is a super simple way of storing fruit for your morning cereals and porridge with no prep time in the morning. It's also a great way to get rid of a fruit bowl full of nearly over-ripe fruit.

- These keep for up to five days in the fridge in an airtight tub.

- You don't have to use Earl Grey: berry teas work really nicely too. Use loose-leaf teas rather than emptying a tea bag as that is too fine to sieve out of the syrup.

Earl Grey Poached Stone Fruits

Serves 4 6

560g caster sugar
875ml boiling water
2 tablespoons Earl Grey
   loose-leaf tea
100g ready-to-eat
   pitted prunes
3 stone fruits (nectarines,
   peaches or apricots),
   stoned and halved
4 plums, stoned and halved

Put your sugar in a pan with the boiling water and the tea leaves. Bring to the boil on the hob and simmer for about ten minutes until syrupy. Take off the heat and pass through a fine sieve to strain out the tea leaves. Put the syrup in a large clean pan and add the prunes, then bring to a simmer for five minutes over a medium heat until the prunes are plump and hydrated. Add the stone fruits and plums and cook for a further five minutes. Remove from the heat and leave to cool. Store in an airtight tub in the fridge and you'll have instant breakfast fruit for the mornings.

Stewed Rhubarb with Orange

Serves 4–6

Rhubarb is very much a spring pleasure. This works really well with brioche and can be used as a filling for the centre of cakes. It is also delicious in a raspberry cake with vanilla frosting. If you want to have lovely red-coloured rhubarb then pop a wee splash of red food colouring into the pan.

· This keeps in the fridge for up to seven days.

400g rhubarb, peeled and
  chopped into 3cm chunks
110g sugar
50ml water
1 orange

Place the rhubarb, sugar and water into a pan with the zest of the orange. Gently cook over a medium heat until the rhubarb is tender enough to put a knife through and the liquid has reduced and become syrupy. Take off the heat, then peel the orange, cut into segments and mix them through the rhubarb. Leave to cool.

Stewed Raspberries

Serves 4

**These make the best topping for French toast, pancakes and porridge.
Also try dropping a few spoons into soda water or bubbly wine – delish!**

· These will keep up to five days in the fridge.

300g raspberries
  (can be frozen)
150g caster sugar
2 tablespoons lemon juice

Place all of the above into a small pan and very gently simmer for 4 or 5 minutes. You want the sugar to dissolve into a syrup, but you also want the raspberries to hold their shape so stop cooking before they break down. Leave to cool.

These apples work really well on granola, porridge, pancakes, natural yogurt, in salads and as a filling for sponge cake with some whipped cream. They are another Mountain Café staple; there is no limit to their uses!

- · Use vanilla sugar (page 293) if you have some, in which case leave out the vanilla pod.

- · These will keep for up to four days in the fridge in an airtight tub.

Vanilla Apples

Serves 4

2 tablespoons lemon juice
60g sugar
2 tablespoons water
1 vanilla pod
2 Granny Smith apples,
  peeled, cored and sliced

Put your lemon juice, sugar and water into a small saucepan. Cut the vanilla pod in half lengthways and scrape all the pulp out into the saucepan, then put the empty pod in too. Add the sliced apples and stir, then gently bring the pan up to a light simmer over a low heat. Cook for about five minutes until the sugar has dissolved and the apples are starting to soften – you need to take them off the heat when they're still a tiny bit underdone as they will finish cooking in the warm liquid. Leave to cool.

Blueberry Compote

Serves 4

Compote is what I think of as a light jam, or fruit cooked in a soft sugary sauce. I love it poured over French toast with lashings of Greek yogurt and honey.

· Store in an airtight jar in the fridge for up to four weeks.

200g frozen blueberries
juice of 1 lemon
¼ teaspoon cinnamon
100ml maple syrup
100g caster sugar

Place the blueberries, lemon juice and cinnamon into a heavy-bottomed pan and bring to the boil. Reduce the heat to a rolling simmer. The blueberries will release quite a bit of juice, so leave to simmer until the liquid has reduced by half. Increase the heat again until the blueberries are boiling and stir in the maple syrup and sugar. Stir until the sugar is completely dissolved – about five minutes. Take off the heat and leave to cool.

Very Berry Compote

Serves 4

A Mountain Café staple from day one. We serve this on our granola and it also gets used on pancakes, cakes and inside muffins.

· Store in an airtight jar in the fridge for up to four weeks.

200g frozen fruits
  of the forest berries
zest and juice of 1 orange
200g caster sugar

Place the berries, orange juice and zest into a heavy-bottomed pan and bring to the boil. Reduce the heat until the berries are at a rolling simmer. The berries will release quite a bit of juice so leave to simmer until the liquid has reduced by half. Increase the heat again until the berries are boiling and stir in the sugar, then cook for about five to ten minutes, stirring, until the sugar is completely dissolved. Take off the heat and leave to cool.

I love this as an alternative to heavy maple syrup: it works great on pancakes and French toast and you can add it to sparkling water as a refreshing summer drink. It is also awesome drizzled over fresh fruit and berries.

· The syrup will keep in a sealed jar in the fridge for a week.

Lime and Mint Sugar Syrup

Makes about 200ml

200ml water
100g caster sugar
zest and juice of 1 lime
8 sprigs mint, stalks removed,
    leaves finely chopped
1 vanilla pod

Place the water, sugar, lime juice and three quarters of the mint into a small pan. Cut the vanilla pod in half lengthways and scrape out all the pulp with a small knife. Put the pulp and the scraped-out pod into the pan. Put onto a high heat and bring to the boil, then reduce to a simmer until the liquid is just starting to thicken – this will take five to ten minutes. Be careful not to let the syrup brown at all. Take off the heat and leave to cool – it will thicken a little bit more. When the syrup is cold, sieve it into a bowl and stir through the remaining mint and the lime zest. Pour into a serving jug or bottle.

Compulsory on warm banana bread and fantastic on pancakes: fire a wee bit in your hot chocolate as a naughty pick me up.

· This will keep in a bottle or jar at room temperature for up to ten days.

· Don't stir when you're making the caramel – just swirl the pan to move the sugar around. Stirring it will cause the sugar to crystallise and become a nasty unusable lump.

Caramel Sauce

Makes 500ml

280g caster sugar
250ml water
90g salted butter
250ml double cream
¼ teaspoon sea salt

Place the sugar and water in a heavy-bottomed saucepan over a high heat. Bring to the boil, swirling the pan often to help with even cooking. Try to resist the urge to stir with a spoon; just let it do its thing. Boil for about 15 minutes, swirling the pan occasionally: the sugar will dissolve into the water to make a clear syrup, which slowly reduces then turns a light amber colour. At this point you need to really start watching – as soon as the syrup becomes an even dark amber you need to remove from the heat and leave on the side for about 30 seconds. This last part will all happen really fast so be ready to whip it off the heat quickly. Carefully drop the butter into the caramel and stir vigorously with a whisk. When it's fully incorporated, add the double cream and again whisk vigorously until you have a smooth glossy caramel sauce. Add the salt, whisk once more and pour into your bottle or jar.

Soup

General Tips for Making Soup

You can use vegetable or chicken stock in any of these recipes – it's up to you. We have kept vegetable stock in the veggie/vegan friendly soups but if you want to use chicken, go for it.

· If you don't have homemade or fresh stock, the general rule I use for stock cubes is: for 900ml to 1 litre of stock, use two stock cubes with 900ml to 1 litre of boiling water; for 1 to 2 litres of stock, use three stock cubes with 1 to 2 litres of boiling water.

· I always look for high quality, preferably organic, stock cubes: then you know they're not full of rubbish and will have less salt and more natural flavour.

· All of these soups can be chilled down after cooking, tubbed and frozen. Make sure they are cold before you freeze them and defrost them in the fridge if possible.

· They will all keep in the fridge for four days once cooked and cooled.

· Finally, it's worth investing in a stick blender for blitzing your soups. It's so much more efficient than pouring it all in a blender!

Stocks

- These will all keep in the fridge for four days in a covered tub.

- If you want to freeze them, leave to cool before putting in a freezer-proof container.

Chicken Stock

Makes 2 litres

If you have roasted a chicken you can use the carcass to make stock; however, you will get a better flavour if you use raw chicken wings or legs.

---

2 medium white onions,
    roughly chopped
1 medium leek,
    roughly chopped
1 medium fennel bulb,
    roughly chopped
1 celery stalk, roughly chopped
1kg raw chicken wings or thighs
6 parsley stalks
6 thyme sprigs
3 rosemary sprigs
4 bay leaves
8 peppercorns
2½ litres water

Place all of the ingredients into a heavy-bottomed soup or stock pot, and bring to the boil over a high heat. Skim off all of the scum that rises to the top, and then turn down to a simmer for three to four hours. Keep skimming any froth that builds up on the top of the liquid. Strain through a sieve lined with a tea towel or muslin cloth to get a lovely clear stock, then leave to cool before putting it in tubs for the fridge or freezer.

Fish Stock

Makes 2 litres

Bones from white fish like sole or turbot are best here – avoid oily fish like salmon or mackerel. Be careful not to over-boil or overcook the stock as it will ruin the flavour.

25g butter

2 medium white onions,
    roughly chopped

1 medium leek,
    roughly chopped

1 medium fennel bulb,
    roughly chopped

2 celery stalks,
    roughly chopped

1kg white fish bones,
    well washed

6 parsley stalks

2 bay leaves

8 peppercorns

2 litres water

Melt the butter in a thick-bottomed soup pan over a medium heat. Add the white onions, leek, fennel and celery and lightly sweat for five to ten minutes. Don't let the vegetables take on any colour – if they do, turn the temperature down. Add the fish bones and sweat for a further five minutes, then add the parsley stalks, bay leaves, peppercorns and water. Bring to the boil and then turn down to a light simmer for 20 minutes, skimming off any foam or froth that rises to the top. Strain through a sieve lined with a tea towel or muslin cloth to get rid of any impurities and leave to cool before putting in tubs for the fridge or freezer.

Veg Stock

Makes 2 litres

Take care not to over-boil or overcook the stock or you will ruin the flavour.

1 tablespoon olive oil

2 medium white onions,
   roughly chopped

2 medium leeks,
   roughly chopped

2 medium carrots,
   roughly chopped

4 thyme sprigs

2 celery stalks,
   roughly chopped

3 garlic cloves,
   roughly chopped

6 parsley stalks

2 bay leaves

8 peppercorns

2 litres water

Heat the olive oil in a thick-bottomed soup pan over a medium heat. Add the white onions, leeks, carrots, thyme and celery and lightly sweat for five to ten minutes. Don't let the vegetables take on any colour – if they do, turn the temperature down. Add the garlic and cook for a couple of minutes, then add the parsley, bay leaves, peppercorns and water. Bring to the boil and then turn down to a light simmer for an hour. Strain through a sieve lined with a tea towel or muslin cloth to get rid of any impurities in the stock, then leave to cool before tubbing up for the fridge or freezer.

Us Kiwis love beetroot, but this is definitely not a Kiwi soup! This one came from Aggie, a crazy Polish chef-lady who worked for us at the café for six years. When she made beetroot soup I thought to myself, 'That will never sell...' But it flew out of the kitchen pass and the customers raved about it.

- Reheat this as quickly as you can and avoid keeping it hot for too long as you will lose the vibrant purple colour.

- This is lovely served with crisp apple slices and horseradish sour cream.

Beetroot and Apple Soup

Serves 4

1½ tablespoons olive oil
1 large onion, roughly chopped
2 Granny Smith apples,
    cored and chopped
    with skin on
1 stick celery, chopped
500g beetroot, peeled and cut
    into equal small even chunks
1200ml vegetable stock
    (or 2 stock cubes in 1200ml
    of hot water)
240ml apple juice
salt
freshly ground black pepper

Heat the oil in a heavy-bottomed soup pan over a medium to high heat and sauté the onion, apple and celery until the onions are translucent and glossy but not coloured. Add the beetroot and stir, then add the stock and apple juice while still on the heat. Cook on a medium heat with a constant fast simmer for about an hour until the beetroot is tender. Blitz until smooth and add a little more hot water or apple juice if the soup is too thick. Season with salt and pepper to taste.

An autumnal butt-kicking, tummy-warming, filling soup for the colder months.

· If you want to make this veggie friendly or don't want to use chorizo then some chopped red peppers make a good alternative.

· Chorizo quite often has gluten in it – check the ingredients if you're making this for gluten free people.

Butternut, Chorizo and Sage Soup

Serves 4–6

550g butternut squash, peeled, deseeded and cut into chunks
2 tablespoons runny honey
4 tablespoons olive oil
1 teaspoon paprika
2 medium onions, roughly chopped
150g chorizo, roughly diced
3 garlic cloves, finely chopped
1 small red chilli, deseeded and roughly chopped
12 sage leaves
1600ml chicken/vegetable stock (or 3 stock cubes in 1600ml hot water)
salt
freshly ground black pepper

Preheat your oven to 200°C (180°C fan).

Put the butternut squash in a roasting tin and drizzle with the runny honey and two tablespoons of the olive oil. Sprinkle over the paprika and some salt and pepper, stir to mix and roast for 20 minutes until the butternut starts to soften. Heat the remaining two tablespoons of oil in a heavy-bottomed soup pot, then add the onions, chorizo, garlic, chilli and sage, and sauté until the onions start to soften and the chorizo has released its oil. Add the roasted butternut squash and the stock. Bring to the boil and simmer on a gentle heat till the butternut squash is very soft – about 40 minutes. Blitz the soup, then season with salt and freshly ground black pepper. If it's too thick for you, add a bit more water. If you have any chorizo left over, cut it into thin slices and crisp them up in a hot pan. Spoon a few slices on top of each serving of soup as a garnish, and I love to drizzle over a little of the hot chorizo oil from the pan for extra flavour.

A simple sexy mushroom soup with an aniseed burst from the fresh tarragon.

· If you don't have any tarragon, try using basil or your favourite herb.

· This is easy to make vegan – just replace the double cream with 400ml stock.

Chestnut Mushroom and Tarragon Soup

Serves 4

2 tablespoons olive oil

2 medium onions,
  roughly chopped

1 big handful fresh tarragon,
  stalks removed

4 garlic cloves, chopped

500g chestnut mushrooms,
  roughly chopped

1200ml vegetable stock
  (or 2 stock cubes in
  1200ml hot water)

400ml double cream

salt

freshly ground black pepper

Heat the olive oil in a large soup pot over a medium-high heat. Add your onions, tarragon and garlic and sauté until the onions start to soften – don't let them take on any colour. Add the mushrooms and sauté for another five to ten minutes till the mushrooms are starting to soften and have reduced in bulk. Pour the stock in, bring to the boil then simmer on a gentle heat till the mushrooms are soft enough to purée (about 30 to 40 minutes). Add your cream and blitz the soup really well until you have a super smooth and creamy texture. Add a little hot water if the soup is too thick, then season with salt, black pepper and extra tarragon if you feel it needs it.

I pinched this recipe off my good foodie friend Queenie – it's damn good, damn quick and damn cheap to make, so put your can opener away!

· Be careful not to overcook this soup so you keep the fresh pea flavour and the vibrant green colour.

· A drizzle of natural yogurt in each bowl is a nice finish.

Chillied Pea and Coriander Soup

Serves 4–6

2 tablespoons olive oil

3 medium onions,
   roughly chopped

1 small red chilli, deseeded
   and roughly chopped

1 big handful coriander,
   stalks and all, roughly chopped

1 big handful mint,
   stalks removed, leaves
   roughly chopped

650g frozen peas

1400ml vegetable stock
   (or 3 stock cubes dissolved
   in 1400ml hot water)

salt

freshly ground black pepper

Put the olive oil in a heavy-bottomed soup pot over a medium-high heat. Add the onions, chilli, coriander and mint and sauté until the onions start to soften. Pour in the frozen peas and the stock, then bring to the boil and simmer over a gentle heat till the peas are soft enough to purée. This will take about 20 minutes at the most. Blitz and add a bit of hot water if it looks too thick. Season with salt and black pepper, and add some more chopped mint and coriander if you feel it needs it.

This is a really sexy fish soup that is a lighter, fruitier take on our fish chowder.

· This is one soup where it's better to use stock cubes rather than homemade stock.

· This will keep in the fridge for four days: put it into a tub once you've blitzed it but before you've added the fish. Then, when you want to eat it, add the fish to the cold soup in the pan and gently reheat it over a medium-low heat. The fish will cook as the soup heats up.

Smoked Fish, Cider and Celeriac Soup

Serves 4–6

50g salted butter

1 medium white onion,
  roughly chopped

1 celery stalk, roughly chopped

1 leek, roughly chopped

2 garlic cloves, chopped

10g dill, roughly chopped

10g chives, roughly chopped

250ml apple cider

2 fish stock cubes

1 small celeriac, peeled
  and cut into small chunks

1 Granny Smith apple,
  unpeeled, cored and cut
  into chunks

1 large potato, peeled and
  chopped into small chunks

1 litre water

250ml double cream

100g smoked haddock,
  cut into 3cm pieces

100g fresh coley (or any other
  white fish), cut into 3cm pieces

salt

freshly ground black pepper

Melt the butter in a heavy-bottomed soup pan over a medium heat. Add the onion, celery, leek, garlic, dill and chives in the butter, and sauté until they begin to soften. Keep stirring and don't let the vegetables take on any colour. Pour over the cider and add the crumbled stock cubes, then leave on a simmer until the liquid has reduced by half. Chuck in the celeriac, apple and potatoes, pour the water over the top and bring to the boil, then turn down to a gentle simmer and leave until the celeriac and potatoes are soft (about 30 to 40 minutes).

Add the cream and blitz until really smooth. Season with salt and freshly ground black pepper. Keeping the soup on a medium-low heat, slide in your pieces of smoked haddock and white fish and gently cook until they are just starting to fall apart. Serve straight away with some crusty bread and maybe a wee chilled glass of cider.

This recipe came from an original Kiwi recipe and has evolved, with many changes along the way, to become the famous Mountain Café Fish Chowder. We took it off the menu one summer and there was local anarchy to the point where we had a couple of angry emails – I'm too scared to take it off the menu again!

· When preparing lemongrass, you want to keep it as a single piece as you need to remove it from the pan before blitzing. Cut it in half lengthways but stop before you get to the bottom, leaving the bulb intact. Then use a small pan or a kitchen mallet to bruise it – this helps let all the flavour out.

· This will keep in the fridge for four days: just put it into a tub once you've blitzed it but before you've added the fish. Then, when you want to eat it, add the fish to the cold soup in the pan and gently reheat it over a medium low heat. The fish will cook as the soup heats up.

Smoked Fish Chowder

Serves 4–6

1 tablespoon olive oil

50g salted butter

1 medium onion, roughly chopped

½ medium carrot,
 roughly chopped

1 celery stalk, roughly chopped

½ leek, roughly chopped

1 handful chives, chopped

1 handful parsley,
 stalks and all, chopped

1 lemongrass stalk,
 almost halved lengthways

1 lemon, zested and halved

175ml white wine

300g potatoes,
 peeled and roughly chopped

1 litre fish stock (or 2 fish stock
 cubes dissolved in 1 litre
 hot water)

250ml double cream

150g fresh salmon,
 skinned and cut into chunks

150g smoked haddock,
 skinned and cut into chunks

4 dill sprigs, chopped

4 strips smoked salmon or
 some thinly sliced fennel
 to garnish

Heat the oil in a heavy-bottomed soup pot over a medium-high heat. Add the butter, onions, carrot, celery, leek, chives, parsley, lemongrass, lemon zest and lemon halves and sauté until the vegetables have started to soften without taking on any colour. Stir in the wine and bring to a rolling boil, then leave, stirring occasionally, until the wine has reduced by a half – about five minutes. Add the potatoes and fish stock and bring back to the boil, then leave to simmer on a medium heat until the potatoes are soft (about 40 minutes). When the potatoes are cooked, use tongs to remove the lemon halves and the lemongrass and discard.

Take off the heat and blitz the chowder until smooth, then add the cream and blitz again. Gently stir in the fish and the dill and put back over a medium-low heat until the fish is just cooked. Serve straight away with each bowl garnished with a strip of smoked salmon or some thinly sliced fennel. Sometimes we finish with a swirl of natural yogurt and a few fennel leaves as well.

This soup is my personal winter favourite; I know the nights are drawing in when this starts making its way back into the kitchen. I love the creamy texture of the parsnips, the sweetness of the honey and the bite from the rosemary.

· A wee drizzle of good quality olive oil looks stunning as a garnish.

· For another classy finish, heat a little vegetable oil in a pan and use your veggie peeler to make some thin parsnip shavings. Drop them into the hot oil and, before they go really brown, scoop them out onto paper kitchen towel to drain and crisp up.

Honeyed Parsnip Soup

Serves 4

2 tablespoons olive oil

2 medium onions,
 roughly chopped

4 rosemary sprigs,
 stalks removed,
 leaves finely chopped

2 garlic cloves, chopped

2 tablespoons runny honey

400g parsnips, peeled
 and chopped into equal
 small chunks

1500ml vegetable stock
 (or 2 stock cubes dissolved
 in 1500ml hot water)

salt

freshly ground black pepper

Heat the oil in a heavy-bottomed soup pot over a medium-high heat. Add the onions, rosemary and garlic and sauté until the onions start to soften. Add the honey and stir to coat the onions, then mix in the parsnips. Pour in the stock, bring to the boil and simmer over a gentle heat till the parsnips are soft enough to purée – about an hour. Blitz the soup, and add a bit more water if it's too thick for your liking: I find that the water often evaporates during cooking and I have to add more hot water as I go. Season with salt and freshly ground black pepper.

Another beast of a recipe from big Kev, our favourite vegan hippy mountain-biking chef! Much to Kev's horror, this soup is awesome with crispy pancetta and Parmesan shavings on top.

· I use a mixture of adzuki, pinto and cannellini beans in this soup but it's up to you what you use. Tinned beans are also fine – just drain and rinse them, then add them into the soup once it's three-quarters cooked so they don't turn to mush.

· Always check packets of dried beans to see if they need to be soaked overnight, rinsed or hardboiled before using. Here are general rules for the beans I use: for cannellini, kidney or blackeye beans, soak overnight, rinse and hardboil for ten minutes; for adzuki or pinto beans, just rinse.

Kev's Bean Soup

Serves 4

140g mixed dried beans,
  soaked and preboiled
  as needed
1 tablespoon olive oil
1 small onion, finely chopped
1 small carrot, finely chopped
1 celery stalk, finely chopped
1 small pepper, deseeded
  and finely chopped
1 small courgette, finely chopped
2 garlic cloves, finely chopped
½ red chilli, deseeded
  and finely chopped
1 handful basil, chopped
1 handful parsley, chopped
1 teaspoon paprika
1 teaspoon cayenne pepper
1 litre vegetable stock
  (or 2 stock cubes dissolved
  in 1 litre hot water)
½ x 400g tin chopped
  tomatoes
salt
freshly ground black pepper

Wash your prepared beans well with fresh water and leave to drain in a sieve while you prepare your veggies. Heat the olive oil in a heavy-bottomed soup pot over a medium-high heat. Add the onion, carrot, celery, pepper, courgette, garlic, chilli, basil and parsley and sauté until everything is glossy and starting to soften but not taking on any colour. Stir in the paprika and cayenne, and cook, stirring, for another couple of minutes. Mix in the drained beans, then pour over your stock and the tinned tomatoes.

Bring up to a light boil for 30 to 40 minutes until the beans are absolutely tender. Season with salt and freshly ground black pepper and some more chopped fresh herbs if you want. I sometimes stir in a spoon of tomato purée at the end to add depth and richness to the soup.

Kumara? What the heck is that? It's sweet potato and it's a staple ingredient that us Kiwis put in everything! This soup is a stunning naturally creamy soup with the ginger and orange cutting through any richness. Delicious.

Kumara, Orange and Ginger soup

Serves 4

2 tablespoons olive oil
1 medium onion,
   roughly chopped
2 garlic cloves, chopped
30g fresh ginger, peeled
   and chopped
2 oranges, zested, peeled
   and chopped
1 handful flat-leaf parsley,
   stalks removed, leaves
   chopped
400g Kumara/sweet potatoes,
   peeled and cut into equal
   small chunks
900ml vegetable stock
   (or 2 stock cubes dissolved
   in 900ml hot water)
salt
freshly ground black pepper

Heat a heavy-bottomed soup pan over a medium-high heat and sauté the onions, garlic, ginger, orange zest and parsley until the onions are clear and glossy but have not taken on any colour. Add the sweet potato and orange flesh and stir it through, then pour in the stock. Keep on a medium heat with a constant rolling boil until the sweet potatoes are tender – this will take about 40 minutes. Blitz until smooth, adding a little more hot water if the soup is too thick, then season with salt and freshly ground black pepper to taste.

A rich and sweet soup with a nice balance of earthiness from the roasted aubergine.

Roasted Red Pepper and Aubergine Soup

Serves 4

1 red pepper, deseeded
  and roughly chopped
3 ripe tomatoes (about 250g),
  roughly chopped
1 small aubergine,
  roughly chopped
5 thyme sprigs, leaves only
2 garlic cloves, peeled and
  left whole
2 tablespoons maple syrup
  (or 20g dark brown sugar)
3 tablespoons olive oil
1 small red onion,
  roughly chopped
1 small white onion,
  roughly chopped
1 big handful fresh basil,
  stalks and all, roughly chopped
1 x 400g tin chopped tomatoes
900ml vegetable stock
  (or 2 stock cubes dissolved
  in 900ml hot water)
3 tablespoons tomato purée
4 basil sprigs, leaves only
salt
freshly ground black pepper

Preheat oven to 200°C (180°C fan). Place the peppers, tomatoes, aubergine, fresh thyme and garlic into a roasting dish and drizzle with maple syrup and a tablespoon of olive oil. Roast till the peppers are starting to soften – about 15 minutes – but make sure you get them out before they brown.

Heat a heavy-bottomed soup pan over a medium-high heat, then add the remaining two tablespoons of olive oil, the onions and the chopped basil. Sauté until the onions are starting to soften, then scrape in the roasted vegetables and sauté for another two to three minutes. Pour in the tinned tomatoes and the veg stock and bring to the boil. Cook on a gentle simmer until the ingredients are soft – about 20 minutes. Add the tomato purée and the remaining basil leaves and blitz with a hand blender till smooth. Add a little more hot water if the soup is too thick and season to taste with salt and freshly ground black pepper.

A smooth sweet potato soup with a refreshing Thai twist.

· To make this vegan, just leave out the fish sauce.

· When preparing lemongrass, you want to keep the lemongrass as a single piece as you're going to remove it from the pan before blitzing. Cut it in half lengthways but stop before you get to the bottom, leaving the bulb intact. Then use a small pan or a kitchen mallet to bruise it – this helps let all the flavour out.

Thai-style Sweet Potato Soup

Serves 6

2 tablespoons olive oil

1 medium onion,
  roughly chopped

2 garlic cloves, chopped

15g fresh ginger, peeled
  and chopped

1 lemongrass stalk,
  almost halved lengthways

3 lime leaves

1 handful fresh coriander,
  stalks and all, roughly chopped
  (plus more for garnish)

2 to 3 tablespoons red
  Thai curry paste (depending
  on how spicy you like it)

400g sweet potatoes,
  peeled and cut into equal
  small chunks

1 x 400g tin of coconut milk

900ml vegetable stock
  (or 2 stock cubes dissolved
  in 900ml hot water)

1 tablespoon dark brown sugar

3 tablespoons fish sauce

1 lime, zested and halved

1 tablespoon desiccated
  coconut (to garnish)

freshly ground black pepper

Heat the olive oil in a heavy-bottomed soup pan over a medium-high heat. Add the onion, garlic, ginger, lemongrass, lime leaves and fresh coriander and sauté until the onions start to soften. Stir in the curry paste, then tip in the sweet potatoes and mix. Pour the coconut milk and stock into the pan and add the brown sugar, fish sauce and the lime zest. Squeeze the lime halves into the soup and then throw in the squeezed halves for good measure.

Bring to the boil and keep at a steady simmer until the sweet potatoes are cooked – roughly 30 to 40 minutes. Use tongs to carefully remove the lemongrass and lime halves and discard them, then blitz the soup until smooth. Add a bit of hot water if it's too thick, then taste and season with more fish sauce and some black pepper if it needs it. Serve with chopped fresh coriander on top and a sprinkle of coconut – I am also a sucker for adding some chopped roasted peanuts and a squeeze of lime juice.

Herbs and KJ's Gardening in Pots

I would love to be able to tell you all how I am this amazing gardening and domestic goddess who grows all my own fruit and veg. At the moment this is a dream for the future: I am often out the door before the sun comes up and get home again in the dark, meaning my husband is the real domestic god in our home.

Much to my late nana and my mum's amusement, my gardening involves a patio full of pots with herbs, rocket, salad, berries and edible plants. I get endless stick from my Kiwi family, how 'That's not a garden, THIS is a garden', as they show off their acre gardens which feed them all year round. But I don't think you have to do back-breaking digging to have a simple selection of tasty herbs, salads and soft fruits. I am a fresh herb addict in all my cooking, but I hate buying fresh herbs from the supermarket and then wasting them because you can't use them all before they go off in the fridge.

There is a simple answer... Pots, pots and more pots! They don't need to be expensive, just simple, free draining pots, tubs or grow bags. Buying a packet of seeds costs less than a herb plant from the supermarket. Drop some potting soil in your pots, plant your seeds, water them daily, feed them occasionally with fertiliser and off you go. Stick them at your back door, in your front room, pop them on your windowsills or even hang them from the kitchen ceiling – I have them all.

I grow soft herbs such as basil, coriander, chives and chervil from seeds in the laundry room so I have them all year round – they will happily grow inside in winter. I leave my rosemary, sage, thyme and mint outside all year and they still provide leaves. My flat-leaf parsley and bay also stay outside in the winter, but I put a strip of frost cloth over them.

Visit your local garden centre for advice and plants, and buy yourself a simple gardening book if you want more detail. You won't regret having fresh herbs at hand for minimal effort and your bank balance will get much less of a hammering when you go to the supermarket!

Here are a couple of my favourite inspirational sites:

· www.boskke.com
  for indoor hanging planters

· www.mytinyplot.com
  for those in the Northern hemisphere

· www.tuigarden.co.nz
  for those in New Zealand

Salads

Building Perfect Salads

BUILDING, LAYERING AND STACKING
It's all in these three words: building, layering and stacking.

Avoid just tipping the salad from your mixing bowl onto your serving dish. When presenting your salad, pick up small handfuls of ingredients and gradually build some height into it, evenly distributing the elements.

If I am making a big platter, I will lay half my dressed salad greens down, scatter half of the ingredients on top and do the same again to get some height. This shows off all the lovely ingredients without hiding them in leaves.

Always dress your salads just before you build them, and then don't let them sit about for too long – they are best served immediately.

ROOM TEMPERATURE IS KEY!
Whenever possible take your ingredients and dressings out of the fridge about an hour before you use them – you'll get a much better flavour. I always take cheeses out of the fridge before using them, and the same with pre-roasted or cooked vegetables. The only exception is salad leaves – I use chilled leaves to avoid them wilting – but all the other components are usually at room temp or even slightly warm. Be a bit careful with rice, pulses and seafood; don't leave them out for long – just long enough to lift the chill off them.

INGREDIENTS
It's all about textures and flavours! If I'm planning a salad I think about the following: crunch, softness, sweetness and zing.

A good example of this is the goats' cheese salad on page 98. We match earthy warmed goats' cheese with crisp, sour Granny Smith apple; sweet blueberries with peppery rocket leaves; tender, cooked green beans with crunchy spiced pecan nuts and spiced blueberry compote with a zingy fruity dressing. It's all about opposites and pairing.

When you're creating a salad, don't use all soft ingredients or all hard ingredients. Here are some examples of opposites that I use: soft creamy cheese with nuts or crisp apple; blue cheese with stem ginger; salty ham with mango or pineapple; chilli with honey and mint; roasted beetroot with lemon juice or a sharp dressing; smoked salmon with radish.

I find this really helps when you're making a salad from scratch.

I had my first encounter with honey mustard dressing when I did work experience for Tracey Ritani in her Katz restaurant in Timaru. Her dressing was perfect in every way – it complimented everything: fish, chicken, spuds, salad. When I started the café I was determined to give customers the same dressing excitement that I had experienced as a teenage pot-washer. It's been part of MC salads since we opened.

· This recipe does make a lot but once you try it, I reckon it will be a fridge door staple. It will keep for six months in an airtight bottle or jar.

· The best way to make this is in a food processor – if you don't have one, follow the same instructions but use a stick blender and a tall jug. Unfortunately if you make it by hand with a whisk it never comes out as silky and is much more likely to split.

· If you're gluten/wheat free, double check the allergy advice on your wholegrain mustard as many brands aren't gluten/wheat free.

Honey Mustard Dressing

Makes 350ml

2 tablespoons
   wholegrain mustard
80ml white wine vinegar
80ml runny honey
1 tablespoon lemon juice
250ml olive oil

Place the mustard, vinegar, honey and lemon juice into your food processor. Turn it on and blitz until all the ingredients are fully combined. With the mixer still running, slowly drizzle in the olive oil. It's really important that you do this slowly and steadily or the dressing will split. Once all the oil is incorporated you should have a thick, glossy, smooth dressing. Pour into a bottle or jar and pop into the fridge.

A dairy-based dressing that's zingy, garlicky and loaded with herbs, it is an essential component for a banging Waldorf salad (page 87).

· This tastes much better if you make it the night before and will keep in the fridge for up to four days.

Ranch dressing

Makes 200ml

80g buttermilk, well-shaken
60g mayonnaise
50g sour cream
1 tablespoon finely chopped
   flat-leaf parsley
½ tablespoon finely chopped
   chives
1 teaspoon finely chopped mint
2 teaspoons white wine vinegar
2 teaspoons lemon juice
½ medium garlic clove,
   finely chopped
salt
cracked black pepper

Put all the ingredients into a bowl and whisk together till thick. Season to taste and put in the fridge.

This is a taste of old school food from the seventies and eighties in New Zealand. Whenever I open my mum's fridge there is always a glass jar of this dressing made up – I eat it with sliced boiled eggs, lettuce, cooked beetroot, tomato and grated cheese. You don't get much more Kiwi than this!

· I included this recipe not just because it's really Kiwi and really tasty, but also because it's a great way of using up any leftover condensed milk from our baking recipes.

· It keeps in the fridge for a week in an airtight jar.

· To make this gluten or wheat free, use cider or white wine vinegar instead of malt.

Old School Kiwi Salad Dressing

Makes about 150ml

100ml condensed milk
60ml malt vinegar
¾ teaspoon mustard powder
pinch of salt
pinch of pepper

Place everything in a bowl and whisk together until smooth and thick. Add more mustard powder and seasoning to taste and if you like a thinner dressing put in a splash more vinegar or hot water.

A tattie salad with a difference – not just boiled spuds with mayo! This salad is bursting with flavours and textures and features the light and zingy Mountain Cafe ranch dressing.

- · You can precook your sweet potato and red peppers – just warm them when you're ready to put your salad together. You can also prepare your feta the day before and leave to marinate overnight.

- · The ranch dressing is best made the night before and will keep in the fridge for four days – the recipe is on page 81.

- · This recipe is really good with some crispy pancetta.

Sweet Potato, Red Pepper, Pine Nut and Feta Salad

Serves 4

500g sweet potato,
  peeled and cut into chunks
5 tablespoons olive oil
1 tablespoon runny honey
2 red peppers, sliced lengthwise
60g pine nuts
200g feta, cut into chunks
10 sage leaves, chopped
1 small chilli, deseeded
  and finely chopped
100g green beans,
  blanched and refreshed
100g mange tout,
  blanched and refreshed
80g good-quality olives
70g rocket
50g spinach leaves
200ml ranch dressing (page 81)
salt
cracked black pepper

Preheat your oven to 200°C (180°C fan). Put the sweet potato in a roasting tray and drizzle with two tablespoons of olive oil and the runny honey. Season with a wee sprinkle of salt and black pepper and mix so everything is evenly coated, then roast for 30 to 40 minutes until just tender. While the sweet potato is cooking, put the red peppers on another tray and drizzle with a tablespoon of olive oil. Season and roast for 20 minutes until they are soft but not browned. Put the pine nuts on a small baking tray and toast in the oven for five minutes to bring out their natural oils and flavour.

Put your feta in a bowl with the remaining tablespoon of olive oil, the chopped sage, chilli and a little cracked black pepper. When you are ready to eat, place the still-warm sweet potato and red pepper in a large bowl and add the marinated feta, toasted pine nuts, green beans, mange tout, olives, rocket and spinach. Dress the salad with as much ranch dressing as you like and season to taste. Serve with a crisp white wine and you will be in heaven.

I'm not really into traditional salads; however this one should be compulsory with the Tartiflette recipe on page 159. It's just a lovely fresh and crisp salad.

· The ranch dressing tastes much better if made the night before. It will keep for up to four days in the fridge.

· Make sure your apples are nice and crisp or they can really ruin the salad.

Waldorf Salad

Serves 4–6

2 Granny Smith apples,
  cored and sliced
200g grapes, cut in half
130g walnuts, toasted
4 celery sticks, finely sliced
70g rocket or salad leaves
200ml ranch dressing (page 81)
salt
cracked black pepper

Put your apples, grapes, toasted walnuts, celery and salad leaves into a large mixing bowl. Pour over all the ranch dressing, season to taste and use your hands to mix through. Serve immediately.

There is a lot of chopping and marinating in this recipe but it is so worth the effort – it's my favourite salad that I've ever created. I am a fresh coriander and mint fiend and this is proven in the recipe – don't scrimp on the fresh herbs or lime!

- The steak needs to be marinated in the fridge overnight.

- If you're making this salad for someone gluten/wheat free, be sure to use free-from soya sauce and swap the egg noodles for rice noodles.

- You can make the different parts of this in advance. As long as you keep them in the fridge, the steak can marinate for up to three days, the dressing will keep for three days and the dressed noodles will be fine for two days.

Beef Salad

Serves 4

---

for the beef:

zest and juice of 4 limes

1 handful coriander,
    stalks and all, chopped

1 handful mint leaves,
    finely sliced

300ml soya sauce

60ml sesame oil

30ml fish sauce

100g brown sugar

40ml rapeseed oil

4 x 200g ribeye or sirloin steaks

a wee spray vegetable oil

salt

freshly cracked black pepper

Make your steak marinade by placing the lime zest and juice into a mixing bowl along with the chopped coriander, sliced mint, soya sauce, sesame oil, fish sauce, brown sugar and rapeseed oil and whisk well. Heat a frying pan or griddle over a high heat until the pan is almost at smoking point, spray with a little bit of oil and put in your steaks. Season with salt and black pepper. Cook the steaks for about three to four minutes each side so they are still pink in the middle. Take off the heat, place the steaks in a tub and pour over the marinade. Leave to cool at room temperature until they are cold enough to go into the fridge, then marinate overnight (or for up to three days).

for the dressing:
200ml reserved beef marinade
30ml red wine vinegar
100ml rapeseed oil

for the noodles:
250g egg or rice noodles
1 tablespoon rapeseed oil
2 tablespoons sesame oil
2 handfuls coriander,
  stalks removed,
  leaves finely chopped
1 handful mint leaves,
  stalks removed,
  leaves finely chopped
1 chilli, deseeded and
  finely chopped
3 spring onions, sliced

for the salad:
150g skinless peanuts
  or cashew nuts
2 teaspoons soya sauce
2 teaspoons fish sauce
1 handful flaked coconut,
  lightly toasted
1 small red onion, finely sliced
1 red pepper, deseeded
  and cut into strips
1 small carrot, peeled
  and super finely sliced
1 cucumber, deseeded
  and sliced into thin strips
1 handful coriander,
  stalks removed,
  leaves roughly chopped
1 handful mint, stalks removed,
  leaves roughly chopped
70g rocket or salad leaves

The next day, drain 200ml of the marinade from the steaks and put it in a small bowl. Add the red wine vinegar and whisk, then keep whisking as you slowly drizzle in the rapeseed oil. The dressing will naturally split if you leave it to sit – this is fine, just give it another little whisk before using.

Cook your noodles according to the instructions on the packet, using a fork to make sure they don't stick together, then drain and refresh in a bowl of cold water. Drain the cold water off the noodles and immediately toss them with the rapeseed and sesame oils to prevent them sticking together. Add the chopped coriander, mint, chilli and spring onion and mix through gently with your hands.

Toast your peanuts or cashews in a small, dry frying pan over a high heat until they are starting to brown, then add the soya sauce and fish sauce on top of the hot nuts and cook for a further minute until they take on all the liquid. Take the pan off the heat.

When you're ready to serve, place your toasted flaked coconut, red onion, red pepper, carrot, cucumber, coriander, mint and rocket/salad leaves in a large bowl. Toss gently to mix the ingredients, then add the noodles and the soya toasted nuts. Drain your steaks, slice them into thin strips and scatter on top. Pour over the dressing, mix gently and serve immediately.

This salad makes for an awesome summer evening meal: it's one of those eat-in-the-garden-while-sipping-a-crisp-glass-of-white-wine numbers.

- To make this gluten and wheat free, make sure you use free-from soya sauce.

- For the best results, marinate the chicken overnight in the fridge. It will keep in there for up to four days.

- You can make the dressing in advance – it keeps for seven days in the fridge.

Let it come up to room temperature before serving. We use Rubicon mango juice in the dressing – replace with orange juice if you can't find it.

- Serve the salad at room temperature to get the maximum flavours from the ingredients.

Coconut Chicken, Mango and Passion Fruit Salad

Serves 4

for the chicken:
400ml coconut milk
2 teaspoons ground coriander
2 tablespoons soya sauce
2 handfuls coriander,
    with stalks, roughly chopped
100g desiccated coconut
zest of 2 oranges
100ml lemon juice
4 chicken breasts, each cut
    into 5 strips lengthways
olive oil
salt
freshly ground black pepper

Place the coconut milk into a large mixing bowl with the ground coriander, soya sauce, chopped coriander, coconut, orange zest and lemon juice. Stir well and season, then add your sliced chicken breasts. Cover the bowl with clingfilm and pop into the bottom of the fridge for at least four hours or overnight if possible – this will give you the most awesome tasting and tender chicken.

To make the dressing, pour the mango juice, lemon juice, passion fruit pulp and sugar into a mixing bowl and whisk. Still whisking, slowly drizzle in the olive oil until it's fully mixed.

for the mango and
passion fruit dressing:
100ml mango juice
70ml lemon juice
pulp of 4 passion fruit
2 teaspoons sugar
170ml olive oil

for the salad:
150g long grain rice,
  cooked and cooled
1 mango, peeled and sliced
  into strips
3 oranges, peeled
  and segmented
100g green beans,
  blanched and refreshed
1 bunch spring onion,
  finely sliced
1 red pepper, sliced
1 green pepper, sliced
100g rocket, washed
1 big handful mint,
  stalks removed,
  leaves finely chopped
1 handful flaked coconut
freshly cracked black pepper

Put the cooked rice into a large mixing bowl with the mango slices, orange segments, green beans, spring onions, sliced peppers, rocket, mint and coconut. Leave out at room temperature while you cook the chicken to bring out all of the flavours.

Preheat the oven to 170°C (150°C fan). Heat a large frying pan and drizzle in just enough oil to coat the bottom of the pan. Take the chicken strips out of their marinade and pan fry on both sides until golden brown, then finish on a baking tray in the oven until cooked right through – about 10 to 15 minutes.

Dress the salad with the mango/passion fruit dressing and a little cracked black pepper, then add the warm chicken strips, quickly but gently tossing the salad with your hands. Layer the salad and chicken into individual serving bowls and eat while the chicken is still warm.

Perfect for a light, fresh, summery lunch or summer's evening salad.

· You can make parts of this in advance: the vanilla pears will keep in the fridge for up to four days, the dressing for up to six days.

· For the best flavour, make the vanilla pears the night before and leave them in the syrup in the fridge overnight.

· Let all the ingredients come up to room temperature before you make the salad.

· Toasted walnuts are a nice addition to this.

Vanilla Pear, Parma Ham and Blue Cheese Salad

Serves 4

for the vanilla pears:
60ml lemon juice
80ml water
1½ tablespoons caster sugar
40ml syrup from the jar
   of stem ginger
1 vanilla pod
2 ripe pears, peeled,
   cored and sliced

for the dressing:
vanilla poaching liquor
juice of 1 lemon
2 tablespoons white wine vinegar
70ml extra virgin olive oil

for the salad:
120g rocket or salad leaves
8 balls of stem ginger,
   drained from syrup
   and finely chopped
2 ripe pears, peeled,
   cored and thinly sliced
300g creamy blue cheese
   (we use Strathdon), crumbled
12 slices Parma ham,
   torn into strips

First, make your vanilla pears. Place your lemon juice, water, caster sugar and stem ginger syrup into a small pan, then scrape in the pulp from the vanilla pod. Chuck the empty vanilla pod in too. Add the sliced pears into the pan, place over a medium heat and gently simmer until the pears start to soften – about seven minutes (use the tip of a sharp knife to check them: they should still be a tiny bit firm as they will continue to cook as they cool). Take off the heat and leave to cool in the pan.

When they're cold, drain the pears, keeping their poaching liquor in a small bowl to make the dressing. Add the lemon juice and white wine vinegar to the bowl and give it a good whisk, then slowly drizzle in the olive oil to make your dressing. The dressing is quite thin and will naturally split, so just give it another whisk before you use it.

Place your washed rocket/salad leaves onto a platter and drizzle with some of the dressing, mixing it through on the platter. Scatter the stem ginger, raw sliced pear, crumbled blue cheese, Parma ham and vanilla pears over the top and give it another decent drizzle of dressing. Serve straight away, so the salad doesn't wilt. A good chunk of crusty bread is a must with this salad.

Baked goats' cheese is one of my biggest weaknesses. I love this salad: I love the passion fruit dressing, the crisp apple slices and the burst you get from the fresh blueberries. It all matches the baked cheese perfectly.

· The spiced blueberry jam will keep for up to one month in the fridge and the dressing will keep for ten days.

· The candied pecans will keep in an airtight container at room temperature for up to three weeks – they also make awesome pre-dinner nibbles.

· The passion fruit syrup is from the recipe on page 286 – if you don't have any you can use a good quality cloudy apple juice instead.

Goats' Cheese, Apple, Candied Pecan and Passion Fruit Salad

Serves 4

for the spiced blueberry jam:
250g frozen blueberries
1 onion, finely diced
50ml red wine vinegar
50g caster sugar
1 teaspoon ground fenugreek
1 teaspoon mustard powder
1 teaspoon ground ginger
1 teaspoon ground cardamom

for the candied pecans:
90g pecan nuts
2 tablespoons icing sugar
½ teaspoon mixed spice
1 tablespoon water

Make the spiced blueberry jam first. In a saucepan place your frozen blueberries, onion, red wine vinegar, caster sugar, fenugreek, mustard powder, ginger and cardamom. Put it over a medium to high heat, bring up to the boil and then turn down to a rolling simmer and cook until the liquid has mostly reduced and you are left with a thickish jam – about 25 minutes. Take off the heat and leave to cool.

Preheat your oven to 170°C (150°C fan). Line a baking tray with some baking paper. Put your pecans, icing sugar, mixed spice and water into a small bowl and mix well before pouring onto the baking tray. Bake for 20 to 25 minutes until the nuts are candied and crisp. Leave the oven on.

for the dressing:

juice of 1 lemon

50ml passion fruit syrup
  (page 286)

60ml white wine vinegar

pulp of 1 passion fruit

1 tablespoon caster sugar

50ml olive oil

salt

freshly cracked black pepper

for the salad:

400g goats' cheese log,
  cut into four thick slices

100g rocket or salad leaves

150g green beans,
  blanched and refreshed

150g fresh blueberries

2 Granny Smith apples, cored

2 Braeburn or red apples, cored

salt

freshly ground black pepper

Next make your dressing. In another small mixing bowl, pour in your lemon juice, passion fruit syrup, white wine vinegar, passion fruit pulp and sugar and whisk to mix. Still whisking, slowly drizzle in your olive oil and season.

Place your slices of goats' cheese onto a baking tray and put into the hot oven until softened and warm – about 10 to 15 minutes. Place your salad leaves in a large bowl with the candied pecans, green beans and fresh blueberries. Just before you take your goats' cheese out of the oven, slice your unpeeled apples into thin slices and add to the bowl of salad ingredients. Drizzle with the dressing, season, mix gently with your hands and pile onto four plates. Place a piece of warmed goats' cheese on top of each salad and finish with a generous spoonful of blueberry jam on top. Eat straight away.

I love lamb; it works really well here with the saltiness of the halloumi cheese, the fresh mint, the bite from the chillies and the sweet orange slices.

· This is also great with the ranch dressing recipe from page 81.

· You can use feta instead of halloumi – just chop it and marinate it, but skip the cooking step.

· The dressing will keep for five days in the fridge.

Seared Lamb, Halloumi, Orange, Roasted Carrot and Almond Salad

Serves 4

for the halloumi:
500g halloumi
2 tablespoons olive oil
1 handful mint leaves, chopped
1 small chilli, deseeded
   and finely chopped
zest of 1 orange (use one
   from the salad ingredients)

for the lamb:
4x200g boneless lamb chops,
   gigots or rump steaks
4 tablespoons olive oil
1 handful sage leaves, chopped
1 handful mint leaves, chopped
3 tablespoons runny honey
cracked black pepper

Slice your halloumi into eight even slices and place on a plate or tray. Drizzle with the olive oil, and then sprinkle over the mint, chilli and orange zest. Cover with clingfilm and put in the fridge for at least two hours (overnight is better) to let the flavours infuse.

Trim your lamb, removing any sinew, bone or excess fat. Place it in a tray or tub and drizzle with the olive oil, then add the sage, mint and honey. Give it a good grind of cracked black pepper and rub all the ingredients into the meat. Cover with clingfilm and put in the fridge for a minimum of two hours (again, overnight is better).

When you're ready to make the salad, preheat your oven to 190°C (170°C fan).

for the salad:

3 raw beetroot, peeled and sliced
  into rounds
4 medium carrots, peeled
  and sliced into chunky fingers
6 tablespoons olive oil
6 tablespoons runny honey
1 big handful mint leaves,
  finely chopped
45g flaked almonds
3 oranges, peeled and sliced
  into rounds
150g green beans,
  blanched and refreshed
10 fresh mint leaves
3 handfuls baby leaf spinach
salt
cracked black pepper

for the dressing:

60ml red wine vinegar
1 small garlic clove,
  finely chopped
1 tablespoon runny honey
1 tablespoon caster sugar
100ml olive oil
salt
cracked black pepper

Make the dressing: whisk together your red wine vinegar, garlic, honey and sugar in a small bowl, then keep whisking as you slowly drizzle in the olive oil. Season to taste. The dressing will seem thin and it will naturally separate – this is fine, just give it another whisk before you use it.

Place your orange slices, green beans, whole mint leaves and baby leaf spinach in a large bowl and let it come to room temperature.

Take your lamb steaks out of their marinade. Heat a dry frying pan, skillet or barbecue to a high heat, then put in the meat and season with salt and black pepper. Cook on both sides till it's done to your liking and place to the side on a warm tray to rest. Heat a non-stick frying pan over a medium to high heat, put in your halloumi slices and cook on both sides until they are golden brown.

Add your still-warm beetroot and carrots to the salad bowl and scatter over the toasted almonds. Dress the salad, toss gently and either split between four individual bowls or layer onto one large platter. Slice your lamb steaks into four or five pieces each and layer on top, then finish with the halloumi and another wee drizzle of dressing over everything. Eat straight away – don't let the halloumi sit around or it starts to toughen.

I pinched this recipe from a friend while I was writing this book. She invited me for dinner and served this incredible chicken dish with an amazing pan of steamed rice and veggies. I stole the idea and put my spin on it by turning it into a salad. So thanks, Lesley Pirie, for inspiring and feeding me when I was exhausted and feeling overwhelmed by writing a book on top of the daily café grind.

· This recipe uses the tabouleh salad from page 111 – make it while the chicken is marinating.

· Use Greek or thick, full fat yogurt – not the runny low fat stuff.

· Marinate your chicken for a minimum of four hours, though overnight is best. The chicken will keep in the marinade in the fridge for up to four days. The dressing will keep in the fridge for up to ten days.

· The chicken makes amazing kebabs for the barbecue.

· The easiest way to get the seeds out of your pomegranate is to cut it in half, hold one half in your hand over a bowl and smack the round side a few times with a rolling pin. The seeds will fall out into the bowl.

· If you can't get or don't like papaya, use mango instead.

Lebanese-style Yogurt, Lemon, Mint and Garlic Chicken Salad

Serves 4–6

for the chicken:
400g Greek or thick,
   full fat yogurt
juice of 3 lemons
4 tablespoons olive oil
2 tablespoons tomato paste
8 garlic cloves, finely chopped
6 coriander sprigs, stalks and all,
   finely chopped
20 mint leaves, finely chopped
4 chicken breasts
cracked black pepper

To make your chicken marinade, place your yogurt into a mixing bowl with the lemon juice, two tablespoons of the olive oil, the tomato paste, garlic, coriander, mint and a good grind of black pepper. Give it all a good stir. Trim any fat, gristle or bone off your chicken breasts and slice each one into three strips lengthwise. Put the strips in the marinade, making sure they're fully coated, then cover with clingfilm and pop in the fridge for a minimum for four hours. While the chicken is marinating, make a batch of the tabouleh on page 111.

Make the dressing: put your lemon juice, honey, white wine vinegar and sugar into a bowl and give it a really good whisk.

for the dressing:
100ml lemon juice
1 tablespoon honey
40ml white wine vinegar
2 teaspoons sugar
120ml olive oil

for the salad:
1 batch of tabouleh (page 111)
1 large papaya, peeled,
  deseeded and sliced
  into strips lengthwise
seeds of 2 pomegranates
1 red pepper, sliced lengthwise
1 small red onion, finely sliced
½ cucumber, deseeded
  and diced
70g rocket or salad leaves

Keep whisking while you slowly drizzle in the olive oil. The dressing will be thin and will split when you leave it – that's fine, just give it another whisk before using it on the salad.

Preheat your oven to 200ºC (180ºC fan). Lift the chicken out of the marinade and discard whatever is left in the bowl. Heat a tablespoon of the remaining olive oil in a large frying pan over a medium-high heat. When it's hot, put in as many of the chicken pieces as you can fit without crowding the pan; you'll need to seal it in a couple of batches – don't throw it all in at the same time. Season lightly with salt and pepper and pan-fry until the pieces are sealed on both sides and lightly browned – about two to three minutes each side. Place your sealed chicken onto a baking tray, and then repeat with the remaining pieces, adding a little more oil if you need it. Once all your chicken pieces are sealed, put them in the oven until they're fully cooked – about 10 to 15 minutes.

Now it's time to assemble your salad! Reserve a quarter of the papaya slices and pomegranate seeds on a plate. Put the rest in a large mixing bowl along with the peppers, red onion, cucumber and rocket or salad leaves. Drizzle with about half the dressing, season with a little salt and pepper and gently toss with your hands. Scatter half of the salad into a large, flattish bowl or platter. Take half of the prepared tabouleh and sprinkle that on top, then top with half of the cooked chicken pieces. Add some more dressing and repeat the layers. Finish the salad with the reserved papaya and pomegranate and a final small drizzle of dressing. Serve immediately.

A fresh minty, citrusy little number that works really well with falafel or lamb koftas and makes a punchy little barbecue salad. It's also a vital part of our Lebanese-style Chicken Salad on page 106.

- To make a gluten or wheat free tabouleh, use buckwheat instead of bulgur wheat. We always use plain buckwheat, not the roasted type, but you can give it a try with either. Rinse 250g buckwheat then put in a saucepan with 375ml water and bring to the boil. Cover and reduce to a very low simmer for 20 minutes. Refresh with cold water and drain.

- The salad keeps in the fridge for up to four days.

- Your bulgur needs to soak in cold water for at least one hour, but you can do it the night before and leave it to soak in the fridge overnight.

Tabouleh Salad

Serves 4

250g bulgur wheat
80ml olive oil
100g kale, stems removed,
   leaves sliced
zest and juice of 1 lemon
zest and juice of 1 lime
½ cucumber, deseeded
   and diced into chunks
3 garlic cloves, finely chopped
1½ bunches mint,
   stalks removed, leaves sliced
1½ bunches flat-leaf parsley,
   stalks removed, leaves
   finely chopped
salt
cracked black pepper

Place the bulgur in a bowl and cover with cold water. Leave it to stand for at least an hour. Put two tablespoons of the olive oil in a large frying pan on a medium-high heat, then add the kale and lightly sauté until it is a vibrant green. Take off the heat. Drain the bulgur and put in a bowl with the lemon zest, lemon juice, lime zest, lime juice, cucumber, garlic, mint and parsley. Give it a good mix, then add the kale and the remaining 50ml olive oil. Season with salt and black pepper to taste, mix really thoroughly and serve.

Boozy poached pears, salty robust blue cheese and sweet hazelnuts with a sharp red wine vinegar dressing: altogether a stylish and extremely flavoursome salad.

· Poach the pears the night before you make the salad so the port can deeply colour and flavour the pears. You can also keep the poaching liquor and reuse it – it keeps for at least a month in the fridge.

· The dressing will keep for up to ten days in the fridge.

· If you are really not into raw veg like mangetout and sugar snaps, just lightly blanch them. I really like them raw as it adds a grassy, nutty flavour.

· Serve everything at room temperature to get the most flavour.

Port-poached Pear, Gorgonzola, Spinach and Hazelnut Salad

Serves 4

for the port-poached pears:
200ml port
200ml red wine
60g Demerara sugar
4 firm pears, peeled,
   cored and quartered lengthwise

for the dressing:
100ml port-poaching liquor
3 tablespoons red wine vinegar
1 tablespoon caster sugar
100ml olive oil
salt
cracked black pepper

for the salad:
130g whole hazelnuts
60g mangetout, finely sliced
100g sugar snap peas,
   finely sliced
100g green beans,
   blanched and refreshed
100g spinach leaves
200g Gorgonzola cheese
salt
cracked black pepper

Place the port, red wine and sugar into a saucepan to make the poaching liquor. Gently warm, then add the quartered pears and make sure they are totally covered in the liquor. Put a circle of greaseproof paper directly onto the poaching liquid to cover the pears and gently simmer till they are three-quarters cooked (i.e. still slightly firm when pierced with a knife). Take off the heat and leave the pears in the pan till cold. We like to leave them in the poaching liquor in the fridge overnight to take on the colour and flavour of the port.

Take 100ml of the poaching liquid and put it in a saucepan over a high heat. Boil for five minutes until it has reduced to a syrupy but pourable consistency. Leave to cool and then tip it into a small mixing bowl. Add the red wine vinegar and sugar and slowly whisk while you drizzle in the olive oil, then season to taste with salt and cracked black pepper.

Smash your hazelnuts up using the end of a rolling pin, then toast the pieces in a dry pan over a medium heat for a couple of minutes – this really brings out the flavour and oils in the nuts. Leave to cool a little.

Drain your poached pears and cut them into thin slices. Put them in a large bowl with the mangetout, sugar snaps, green beans and spinach. Scatter over the toasted hazelnuts and drizzle everything generously with dressing. Season with salt and black pepper, then gently toss the salad with your hands and put on a serving platter or into individual bowls. Slice the gorgonzola over the top and serve immediately.

Not just a summer salad! This is a healthy, feel-good salad, loaded with fresh goodness.

· The salmon needs to marinate for at least four hours, preferably overnight.

· As an alternative, you could use smoked salmon instead of fresh and marinate it as per the recipe.

· Make this wheat free and gluten free by using free from soya sauce.

· We use wasabi powder and hydrate it as we need it. It's less in your face than other types and stores really well. If you can't get the powder, then use the same amount of pre-prepared wasabi paste.

· If you're not keen on grapefruits, blood oranges are also magic in this salad. Your dressing will keep for five days in the fridge.

Salmon Salad

Serves 4

---

for the salmon:

4 salmon fillets, skin on

3 tablespoons olive oil

zest of 1 grapefruit

1 handful dill, stalks removed, leaves finely chopped

1 chilli, finely diced

for the noodles:

200–250g rice noodles

1 tablespoon sesame oil

40ml soya sauce

2 handfuls coriander, stalks removed, leaves finely chopped

1 handful mint, stalks removed, leaves finely chopped

1 chilli, deseeded and finely chopped

Place your salmon fillets skin down on a tray or plate and drizzle with the olive oil. Sprinkle the grapefruit zest, dill and chilli evenly over each fillet, then cover with clingfilm and pop in the fridge for at least four hours to take on the flavours.

Drop your rice noodles into a pan of boiling water, cook until they have just softened, drain, refresh in cold water and drain again. Put in a large bowl and, using your hands, toss immediately with the sesame oil and the soya sauce to prevent the noodles drying out or sticking together. Toss in the coriander, mint and chilli.

To make the dressing, put your wasabi powder in a small mixing bowl and stir in the water to make a smooth paste. Add the sugar, soya sauce, rice wine vinegar, sesame oil and lemon juice and whisk together. Still whisking, slowly drizzle in the rapeseed oil till you have a glossy thick dressing.

for the dressing:

8g wasabi powder

25ml water

2 teaspoons caster sugar

25ml soya sauce

30ml rice wine vinegar

20ml sesame oil

1 teaspoon lemon juice

50ml rapeseed oil

for the salad:

2 grapefruits, peeled
  and segmented

2 tablespoons caster sugar

8 radishes, trimmed
  and thinly sliced

75g fresh peas

1 handful cress

150g mangetout

1 bunch asparagus,
  blanched and refreshed

6 baby corn, blanched
  and refreshed

4 spring onions, finely sliced

Place your grapefruit segments in a small bowl and sprinkle with the sugar. Put the radishes, peas, cress, mangetout, asparagus, baby corn and spring onions into a large mixing bowl and toss to combine. Drain any liquid off the grapefruit and add them to the bowl as well.

Preheat your oven to 200°C (180°C fan). Heat a large non-stick frying pan over a high heat. Very lightly oil your pan by rubbing a little olive oil on with kitchen towel. Gently put in the four salmon fillets, skin side up, and cook until golden brown, then gently flip them over and put them in the oven for about ten minutes until they are cooked through.

Drizzle plenty of dressing over the bowl of radishes and peas, etc, and toss gently to combine. Place half of the noodles on a large platter, then scatter half of the dressed salad on top. Repeat the layers with the remaining noodles and salad, then put the salmon fillets on top. Finish with a little more dressing and eat straight away.

Gin in a salad – it has to be a winner! The citrus and gin marinade gently cooks the raw salmon, and combines with a zingy dressing, earthy beetroot and juicy brambles for a fresh, light and subtle salad.

- The sloe salmon needs at least four hours in the marinade so it cooks in the citrus. For the best results, leave it in overnight – it will be fine in the fridge for up to four days.

- Either slice your fennel at the last minute or lightly coat it in lemon juice to stop it going brown.

- The dressing will keep for up to ten days in the fridge.

Sloe Gin and Bramble Salmon Salad

Serves 4

---

for the sloe salmon:
75ml gin
100ml sloe gin
75g frozen blackberries
40g sugar
zest and juice of 2 oranges
75ml lemon juice
5 sprigs dill, stalks removed, leaves finely chopped
300g fresh salmon fillet, skinned, pin-boned and sliced into thin strips
200g hot-smoked salmon, skinned and flaked

To make your sloe salmon marinade, place your gin, sloe gin, frozen blackberries and sugar in a saucepan. Bring to the boil over a medium-high heat until the sugar has dissolved and the liquid has had a really good boil – about five to six minutes. Take it off the heat and blend in a food processor until smooth, then sieve into a mixing bowl and discard all of the seeds and pulp left behind in the sieve. Add the orange zest, orange juice, lemon juice and dill and whisk, then gently put the fresh and smoked salmon pieces into the marinade. Mix so all the pieces are well covered and leave in the fridge for at least four hours, preferably overnight.

for the salad:

3 beetroot, peeled
  and thinly sliced
2 tablespoons olive oil
1 tablespoon runny honey
¾ cucumber, deseeded
  and thinly sliced
1 small fennel, super finely sliced
1 packet cress, snipped
4 spring onions, sliced into
  fine matchsticks
150g fresh brambles
50g pea shoots
60g salad leaves, washed

for the dressing:

zest and juice of 1 lime
50ml sloe gin
50ml red wine vinegar
1½ tablespoons caster sugar
50ml olive oil
salt
freshly cracked black pepper

Preheat your oven to 200°C (180°C fan). Put your beetroot in a small roasting tray with the olive oil and honey, season with salt and pepper and mix with your hands to make sure the slices are evenly coated. Roast until the beetroot is tender enough that a knife will go through the slices easily – roughly 20 minutes. Cover with tin foil and leave to cool.

To make the dressing, place your lime zest and lime juice in a small bowl with the sloe gin, red wine vinegar and sugar. Give it a whisk and keep whisking as you slowly drizzle in the olive oil. The dressing will seem a bit thin and will split as it sits – just give it another mix before using on your salad.

Now you just have to put everything together. Scoop all the salmon out of the juices and put into a large salad bowl. Add your roasted beetroot along with the cucumber, fennel, cress, spring onion, brambles, pea shoots and salad leaves. Drizzle over the dressing and season with salt and cracked black pepper, then gently but thoroughly toss with your hands. Serve immediately.

This is my 'I've had a huge day at work, but I don't want to eat a takeaway' meal. It's so quick, simple and healthy – I love it! Add some grilled chorizo and drizzle the hot oil from the pan over the salad for a naughty finish.

- Use the best, ripest, nicest tomatoes you can get your hands on.

- Pick up decent extra virgin olive oil and balsamic glaze from a good deli or Italian shop.

Super-fast but Super-sexy Tomato and Mozzarella Salad

Serves 1 hungry person

1 buffalo mozzarella ball,
  drained and sliced
8 fresh basil leaves
1 beef tomato, cored and
  thinly sliced
8 cherry tomatoes, halved
1 vine plum tomato,
  cored and thinly sliced
¼ small red onion,
  super finely sliced
extra virgin olive oil
good quality balsamic glaze
sea salt
cracked black pepper

It's so simple – just layer all your tomatoes, mozzarella and basil onto a plate, seasoning with sea salt and cracked black pepper as you go. Make it look sexy! Drizzle with as much olive oil as you fancy and the same with the balsamic glaze and eat. My kind of fast food!

Mains

These fragrant fritters are great as a light meal, or as part of a picnic – give them a squeeze of fresh lime juice and some flaked coconut and chopped fresh coriander when serving.

· Sweet potatoes work just as well here as butternut squash. To make a gluten/wheat free version, just use free-from self-raising flour.

· When I make these at home, I get three or four fritters in the pan at one time so you might want to have two pans on the go at once as you will get eight fritters out of the batter. If you're only using one pan, keep the first batch warm in a 140°C oven.

· The batter keeps for up to two days in the fridge – if it looks a bit runny when you come to use it, add a little more self-raising flour.

Butternut, Peanut, Chilli and Coconut Fritters

Serves 4–6

500g butternut squash, peeled, deseeded and cut into 2cm dice
1½ tablespoons olive oil
2 garlic cloves, finely chopped
1 small red chilli, de-seeded and finely chopped
2 handfuls coriander, stalks removed, leaves finely chopped
1 bunch spring onions, finely chopped
130g crunchy peanut butter
40g desiccated coconut
zest of 2 limes
80g ground almonds
4 large eggs
100g self-raising flour
salt
cracked black pepper

Preheat your oven to 200°C (180° fan).

Put your butternut squash in a roasting tray and drizzle with a tablespoon of the olive oil. Season with salt and pepper and roast for 20 minutes until the squash is tender enough to mash but not browned. Roughly mash it in the tray, then scrape it into a large mixing bowl with the garlic, chilli, coriander, spring onion, peanut butter, coconut, lime zest, ground almonds and eggs. Mix together until you have a smooth batter, then add the flour and season well to taste.

Heat the remaining olive oil in a non-stick frying pan over a medium heat. Once it's good and hot, spoon your batter into the pan – we make our fritters about 8cm in diameter. Cook on either side until fluffy and cooked through in the middle and golden brown and crisp on the outside – about seven minutes on each side should do it. Serve immediately, with some salad and a big glass of chilled wine.

An absolute Kiwi classic. Healthy, light and tasty, these bad boys are great for any time of day or night. They are excellent cold as a snack or in packed lunches too.

· Make these dairy free by leaving out the sour cream.

· Sometimes I like to garnish with a light drizzle of sweet chilli sauce.

· Try them with bacon, avocado and our slow roasted tomatoes (page 35) as a brunch/breakfast dish – amazing! The batter will keep for eight hours in the fridge.

· These make really cool wee canapés.

Sweetcorn Fritters

Serves 4

1x340g tin sweetcorn in brine

1 small red onion, finely diced

1 red pepper, finely diced

1 small courgette, grated

1 small sweet potato,
  peeled and grated

3 spring onions, finely
  sliced into thin rounds

1 small red chilli, finely diced
  (leave the seeds in if you
  like a kick)

1 handful coriander,
  stalks removed,
  leaves roughly chopped

zest and juice of 1 lemon

2 large eggs

1 tablespoon sweet chilli sauce

2 teaspoons salt

1½ teaspoons black pepper

200g self-raising flour

2 teaspoons olive oil

100ml sour cream

a handful salad leaves

400g hot smoked salmon

honey mustard dressing
  (page 80)

Tip your tin of sweetcorn and its brine into a large bowl with the red onion, red pepper, courgette, sweet potato, spring onion, chilli, coriander and lemon zest and juice and mix until thoroughly combined. Crack your eggs into the bowl and add the chilli sauce, salt, and pepper and mix again. Fold in the flour until you have a thick spoonable batter.

Preheat a non-stick pan over a medium heat, drizzle in a teaspoon of the olive oil and use a paper kitchen towel to wipe it over the base of the pan. Now drop large spoonfuls of batter into the hot pan – you need to get 12 fritters out of your mix to serve four people, so we make them about 7cm in diameter. Gently cook on both sides till golden brown, flipping as little as possible. When you think they are ready, gently break one apart to check the inside is cooked. Re-oil the pan if you need to and repeat with the rest of the batter.

Lay out four fritters on a platter. Spoon some sour cream onto each one, then add a few salad leaves and a piece of smoked salmon and drizzle with a little honey mustard dressing. Put another fritter on top of each one to make a stack and add another layer of fillings. Finish with a third fritter and serve – if your stacks look precarious, use a skewer to hold them together.

I can still remember the first time I had bacon and egg pie. I was about six; a friend from school invited me to go with her parents on a vintage car rally. Her mum was an incredible cook and at lunch time she pulled out these huge slabs of heaven. We sat on a rug and I will never forget the smoky, salty, eggy heaven that was served that afternoon.

· You need a deep dish for this, to hold all the filling.

· This will keep in the fridge for four days after baking.

· To reheat, give each piece a minute in the microwave and then pop into a preheated oven at 180°C (160° fan) till hot in the centre.

Bacon and Egg Pie

Serves 6

250g puff pastry
plain flour for dusting
6 smoked bacon rashers, diced
1 small red pepper, diced
1 small green pepper, diced
1 medium red onion, diced
75g garden peas (frozen are fine)
1 handful coriander,
  stalks removed, leaves chopped
1 handful parsley,
  stalks removed, leaves chopped
120g Cheddar, grated
6 eggs
200ml double cream
1 teaspoon sea salt
2 teaspoons cracked
  black pepper

23 x 23 x 5cm square pie dish

Preheat oven to 180°C (160°C fan) and grease your pie dish.

Have your pastry at room temperature to make it easier to roll. Sprinkle a little flour onto your bench and rolling pin, and roll the pastry out to a large enough square to fit the dish. Press it into the dish and leave for 20 minutes to rest, then trim any excess pastry from the edges.

Put the bacon in a bowl with the peppers, onion, peas, coriander, parsley and Cheddar and mix together with your hands. Place in an even layer in the pastry-lined dish. Whisk the eggs, cream, salt and pepper till smooth, then slowly and carefully pour over the filling in the dish. Gently put it into the oven to bake for 1 hour 10 minutes till the filling is golden and just firm to the touch.

This recipe was inspired by a recipe that I cooked in the New Zealand culinary competitions. It started its life as a sexy wee tart, served with Kiwi venison and a rich jus, and won our team from Aoraki Polytech a gold medal at the Junior Team Skills competition. It has evolved over time and is now a quiche that we sell truckloads of – it has fuelled many an outside catering function too.

- It is important to finish with a top layer of sweet potato on the quiche to protect the spinach from burning in the oven.

- This keeps in the fridge for four days. To reheat, give it a minute in the microwave and then finish it off in a 180°C (160°C fan) oven until it's hot all the way through.

Sweet Potato, Spinach and Caramelised Onion Quiche

Serves 6

for the base:
200g puff pastry
plain flour for dusting

for the filling:
2 large white onions,
   peeled and thinly sliced
25g salted butter
a splash of olive oil
30g dark brown sugar
6 large eggs
300ml double cream
2 teaspoons nutmeg
1 teaspoon sea salt
1 teaspoon cracked
   black pepper
60g spinach
2 medium sweet potatoes,
   peeled and cut into
   5mm slices

23cm loose-bottomed tart tin

Preheat your oven to 180°C (160°C fan) and grease your tin.

Have the pastry at room temperature so it is easy to roll. Sprinkle a little flour onto your bench and roll out the pastry until it is large enough to line the tin and about 2mm thick. Place and press into the prepared tin and leave to rest on the side for 20 minutes. Trim any excess pastry off the edges.

While the pastry is resting, place the sliced onions into a frying pan with butter and olive oil. Sauté on a medium heat until they are translucent and soft (about 10 minutes). Turn the heat down. Sprinkle the brown sugar over the onions, stir through and cook gently until the onions are syrupy and caramelised (about 5 minutes). Leave to cool, then tip the onions into a sieve to drain off any liquid.

Whisk the eggs, double cream, nutmeg, salt and black pepper together in a large bowl. Put the cooked and drained onions in a layer on the pastry and cover with half of the spinach then a layer of sweet potato slices. Add another layer of spinach and finish with the remaining sweet potato – remember that sweet potato needs to be on the top as the spinach will burn. Slowly pour the egg mix over the filling, taking your time so it soaks right through and doesn't pour over the edges. Bake for 50 minutes until the top of the quiche is firm to touch and no egg mix oozes out when a knife is stuck into the middle.

Laura, our lovely Irish chef, came up with this recipe for an evening do we were cooking at. They are simple, tasty, light and fresh – and so good that carnivores often order them instead of their meat fix.

· If you don't have wee pie dishes you could use muffin pans instead; make two per portion instead of one.

· You can prep all the ingredients and cook the squash in advance – get your pastry cases ready too. Then when you're ready to eat, just pull everything out, bind it, fill the cases and bang them in the oven. They're a great quick dinner once the prep is done.

· The tarts aren't great for reheating – you really need to eat them straight away – but they are nice cold in a packed lunch the next day.

Laura's Veggie Tarts

Serves 4

200g puff pastry
250g butternut squash,
    peeled and chopped into
    2cm cubes
2 tablespoons olive oil
1 large red onion, halved
    and thickly sliced
1 red pepper, roughly chopped
1 big handful basil,
    stalks removed, leaves sliced
40g spinach, thinly sliced
150g feta cheese
200g crème fraîche
salt
cracked black pepper

4 x 10cm tart tins

Take your pastry out of the fridge and let it sit at room temperate to soften. Preheat your oven to 180°C (160°C fan).

Place your chopped butternut squash into a small roasting dish and drizzle with a tablespoon of olive oil and a wee sprinkle of salt and black pepper. Bake for about 15 to 20 minutes, until the butternut squash is cooked through. Leave to cool.

Heat the remaining tablespoon of olive oil in a pan and add your red onions. Lightly sauté, stirring in the red peppers when the onions are half cooked, then cook until everything has softened. Leave to cool.

Grease your pie dishes and flour your work top. Roll out the pastry into a rough square 2mm thick, then cut into four equal pieces and line the tins. Put the onions, red peppers and butternut squash in a bowl and add the basil and spinach. Crumble the feta into big chunks on top, season to taste and then gently fold the crème fraîche through the vegetable mix. Pile into the waiting tins, dividing the mix equally four ways.

Bake for 35 to 45 minutes until the pastry is golden brown and the filling is bubbling and hot. Serve straight away with salad, crusty bread and a glass of vino.

Black pudding with fresh chilli, sage and crisp chunks of apple in buttery crisp filo pastry = total heaven served straight from the oven.

· Instead of making rectangular parcels, you could line large muffin tins with the filo, then put in a ball of the black pudding filling and scrunch up the filo on the top to make a pie. Make sure you grease and flour the tins and use plenty of butter inside and outside the parcels.

· You can freeze the black pudding filling, but I wouldn't freeze the made-up filos as they will go soggy.

· These will keep in the fridge for three days, uncooked. Don't stack them on top of each other as they'll stick together – store them on a tray lined with greaseproof paper and covered with clingfilm.

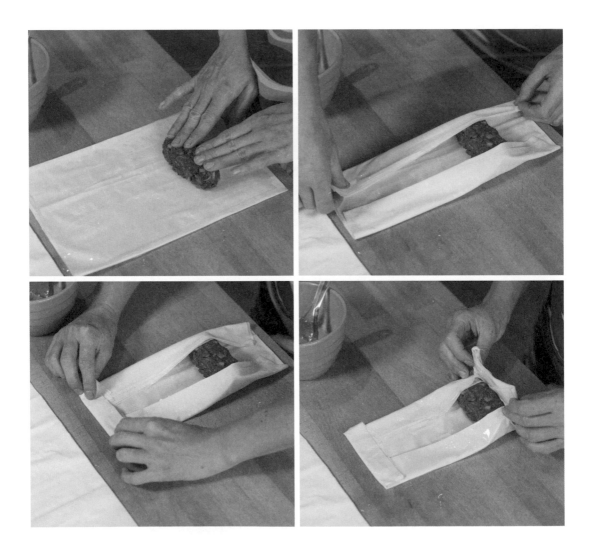

Black Pudding, Apple and Sage Filos

Serves 4

400g good quality
  black pudding, thickly sliced
1 cooking apple,
  grated with skin on
1 Red Delicious apple, peeled
  and chopped into wee chunks
1 small red pepper, diced
1 medium red onion,
  finely chopped
1 small chilli, finely chopped
  (with seeds if you like
  a spicy kick)
1 large handful sage,
  stalks removed,
  leaves finely chopped
2 x 270g packets filo pastry
250g butter, melted
2 tablespoons poppy
  or sesame seeds

Preheat your oven to 180°C (160°C fan). Lightly grease and flour a baking tray.

Place the black pudding in a roasting dish with no oil. Cook in the oven for about 15 minutes until it is three-quarters cooked. You don't want it fully cooked at this stage or it will be dry and hard to work with. When it's cool enough to handle, crumble into a large mixing bowl. Add the apples, red pepper, onion, chilli and sage and mix together with your hands. Split the mixture into eight even pieces, and then roll each one into a fat sausage about 10cm long – it will be easier to shape these if the black pudding is still a little warm.

Unwrap the filo onto a dry, clean bench. Start by placing two filo sheets on top of each other, with the short edge in front of you. Brush generously with melted butter, then take one of the black pudding sausages and put it on the pastry so it's parallel to the edge nearest you, about 5cm in. Fold in the left and right sides of the pastry so they meet in the middle over the black pudding.

Brush again with plenty of butter. Roll the pastry up from the edge nearest to you to form a parcel, applying a bit of pressure towards the end to seal it, then brush the top with more butter and sprinkle with poppy or sesame seeds. Repeat with the remaining filo and black pudding to make eight neat little packages. If your filo starts to dry out, lay a clean, damp tea towel over the pastry.

Bake for around 20 minutes until golden brown. Serve with salad or a wee apple salsa. Honey mustard dressing (page 80) goes really well, as does sweet chilli dipping sauce.

From the day we opened I was determined not to buy in processed, cheap or pre-made burgers. I wanted to know exactly what went into them, so they would always be consistent, delicious and not full of rubbish. I think we've nailed them!

· Don't skip cooking the onions and garlic: the raw onion will make the burgers fall apart.

· Be really hands-on when you're making them – really work the meat to make sure everything is fully bound, as this will help them hold together.

· Use lean and fresh butcher's mince – the more fat and rubbish in the meat, the less tasty and more greasy your burgers will be, and the more likely they are to fall apart.

· This recipe is best cooked in a hot pan. They don't really work on a barbecue grill, unless you have a hot plate.

· We use the same mix to make meatballs.

· You can freeze the burgers, but they are more likely to fall apart when you defrost and cook them.

Beef Burgers

Serves 4

1 medium onion, very,
  very finely chopped
2 garlic cloves,
  finely chopped or grated
½ teaspoon dried mixed herbs
¼ teaspoon olive oil
600g freshly ground beef mince
2 teaspoons wholegrain mustard
2 teaspoons paprika
2 teaspoons ground cumin
3 tablespoons chopped parsley
2 tablespoons chopped coriander
2 teaspoons sea salt
1 teaspoon cracked black pepper

In a small frying pan, lightly cook the onion, garlic and mixed herbs in the olive oil until the onions are translucent but have not taken on any colour. Remove from the heat and leave to cool. Put your mince in a large bowl with the wholegrain mustard, paprika, cumin, parsley, coriander, salt and black pepper. Add the cooled, cooked onions. Using your hands, mix the ingredients through the mince – you really need to work this hard to get a good mix; don't be wishy washy – really give it laldy. Split the mince into four equal pieces and again really work each one to get a smooth firm ball.

Flatten and shape in your hand to make four big burgers, then place on a plate, cover in clingfilm and leave in the fridge for an hour or so to rest.

Heat a large frying pan over a medium heat – if the pan is too hot you will burn the outside and the middle will be raw, so you want an even heat that will seal the burgers but not burn them. Cook on both sides until done: they will take about 15 to 20 minutes to cook through. Alternatively, brown the outside of the burgers then pop into a preheated oven at 200°C (180°C fan) until they are cooked through – they won't be as juicy this way though.

Serve with a good quality bun and all your favourite burger trimmings and the job's a good 'un!

Light and refreshing Middle Eastern kebabs, packed full of flavour and really good with our fresh tabouleh salad (page 111) and tzatziki (page 281). I also love them crammed in a pitta bread with hummus and salad.

· If you are barbecuing the kebabs, soak your sticks in water overnight so they don't catch fire.

· The uncooked kebabs will keep in the fridge for four days, and freeze quite well – I would individually wrap them in clingfilm first. They are more likely to fall apart when cooking if they've been frozen, but they'll still taste good.

· Once cooked you need to eat them within two days – but they're best if they're cooked and eaten fresh.

Lamb Kofta Kebabs

Serves 4

¼ teaspoon olive oil

1 medium white onion,
very, very finely chopped

3 garlic cloves, finely chopped
or grated

20 mint leaves, chopped

1 medium chilli, finely chopped
(leave seeds in if you like
a bang)

800g lamb mince

1 big handful coriander, stalks
removed, leaves chopped

2 teaspoons paprika

2 teaspoons ground cumin

1 teaspoon turmeric

zest of 1 lemon

2 teaspoons salt

1 teaspoon cracked black pepper

12 kebab sticks

Put the olive oil in a pan over a low heat. Add the onion, garlic, just under half of the mint and the chilli and sauté until the onions are translucent but not browned. Leave to cool.

Place the lamb in a large bowl and add the remaining mint and the coriander, paprika, cumin, turmeric, lemon zest, salt and cracked black pepper. Tip in the cooled onions and, using your hands, mix the ingredients really thoroughly into the mince – you must be quite forceful. Split into 12 equal pieces and again really work each one with your hands to get a smooth, firm ball. Put a strip of clingfilm down on the bench and roll each ball on it to make a sausage. Flatten between your palms, then stick a kebab skewer down the middle and shape the meat around it. Place the kofta on a tray, cover in another piece of clingfilm and leave in the fridge for an hour or so to rest.

Heat a dry frying pan over a medium heat – if the pan is too hot you will burn the outside and the middle will be raw, so you want an even heat that will seal the kofta but not burn them. Cook on both sides until browned and crispy on the outside and cooked through inside – they will take about 10 to 15 minutes. Alternatively, brown the outside of the kofta in the pan then pop into a preheated oven at 200°C (180°C fan) until they are cooked through – they won't be quite as juicy though.

Adam is a chef from the Borders who was with us in the early days and he was our karaoke clean-down king. Whenever he was working, there was an amazing buzz of lovely food and crazy French tunes bouncing around the kitchen. These fish cakes were Adam's signature dish at the café, and they're incredible.

· Use whatever white fish you like: haddock, hake, cod, halibut and coley are all good options.

· You can make these gluten or wheat free by using appropriate breadcrumbs and free-from flour.

· The uncooked fish cakes will keep in the fridge for three days.

· Once cooked, they are best eaten straight from the pan as they don't freeze or reheat very well.

Adam's Fish Cakes

Serves 6

for the fish cakes:
375g Maris Piper potatoes,
    peeled and roughly chopped
50ml double cream
25g butter
1 teaspoon olive oil
½ red onion, finely chopped
1 garlic clove, finely chopped
½ lemongrass stalk,
    finely chopped
2 tablespoons fish stock
½ teaspoon finely chopped
    rosemary
400g mixed white fish,
    skinned and boned
1 bay leaf
500ml full fat milk
25g smoked salmon,
    roughly chopped

Boil your potatoes in a large saucepan until they're just cooked through. Drain them, place them back in the pan, and mash them with the double cream and butter until smooth. Set to the side to cool.

Heat the olive oil in a frying pan over a medium heat. Add the red onion, garlic and lemongrass and sauté until the onions are soft and translucent. Turn the heat up to high, add the fish stock, and cook for a minute until the stock has reduced and is absorbed into the onion mix. Add in the chopped rosemary and leave to cool, then stir it through the mashed potato.

½ teaspoon finely chopped
    chives
½ teaspoon finely chopped dill
salt
cracked black pepper

for the crumb:
50g plain white flour
200g white breadcrumbs
1 egg
150ml full fat milk
250ml vegetable oil for frying

Lay the white fish and bay leaves in a heavy-bottomed saucepan and pour over the milk. Cover with a lid and bring to the boil over a high heat, then take off the lid and reduce to a simmer for four minutes. Take the pan off the heat and let it stand for ten minutes to gently finish cooking the fish in the hot milk. Lift the fish out of the pan with a slotted spoon and put on a plate to cool. Once cool, add it to the mashed potato along with the smoked salmon, chives and dill, and add some salt and cracked black pepper. Mix through until fully combined, then split the mix into 12 evenly-sized balls. Flatten each one between your palms to make cakes about 3cm thick. Place on a tray or plate and leave in the fridge for at least two hours.

Once the fish cakes are chilled they can be crumbed. Put your flour in one shallow bowl, your breadcrumbs in another and whisk the eggs and milk together in a third. Dip each fish cake in the flour so they are completely covered, then shake off any excess and dip them in the egg wash. Finally, roll them in the breadcrumbs, squeezing them so they are tight and evenly crumbed.

Preheat your oven to 210°C (190°C fan). Put the vegetable oil in a large frying pan over a medium-high heat and let it get hot – if a piece of bread sizzles when it's dropped in, it's hot enough. Gently slide in three or four fish cakes at a time and fry them for four to six minutes on each side until golden brown and crisp all over. Then place them onto a baking tray and put into the oven for about ten minutes until they are hot in the middle.

Serve with fresh lemon wedges, tartar sauce and a rocket salad.

This recipe has been the toughest recipe yet to convert to household measures: we make batches of 160 at a time in the café and then freeze them down, defrosting what we need each day. Finally we have mastered this recipe to make 12, and they taste exactly the same as the ones on our menu. I hope you enjoy!

- If you don't have a food processor, finely chop the vegetables and then use a pestle and mortar to get a smoothish paste.

- You could use tinned or frozen corn kernels, but I really love the crunch of the raw corn straight from the cob.

- To test the seasoning, we make a very small burger first, cook it and taste it.

The raw mixture should be very well-seasoned.

- These burgers are really handy to have in the freezer: they take two hours to defrost, so they are great as an emergency back-up meal when you're short for time. Wrap individually in clingfilm before you freeze them.

Veggie Burgers

Makes 12 burgers

100g black beans
  (or 180g cooked weight)
100g red lentils
150g puy lentils
100g brown rice
2 veggie stock cubes
700ml water
4 garlic cloves, peeled
1 chilli, roughly chopped
80g coriander, stalks and all
35g ginger, peeled and
  roughly chopped
2 tablespoons olive oil

Put your black beans in a pan with plenty of water and bring to the boil over a high heat. Cook over a rolling simmer for about 40 to 50 minutes until they're tender – you may need to top up the water as they cook as they're quite thirsty. Drain and rinse with cold water until the water stops running black.

Put your red lentils in a large, heavy-bottomed pot with the puy lentils, brown rice and vegetable stock cubes. Pour over 700ml water and bring to the boil. Cook over a medium heat, stirring, until the lentils and rice are three-quarters cooked and most of the water is absorbed. While they're cooking, place your garlic, chilli, half the fresh coriander, the ginger and a tablespoon of the olive oil into a food processor and

1 red onion peeled,
  halved and finely sliced
1 white onion peeled,
  halved and finely sliced
1 carrot, peeled and grated
½ sweet potato,
  peeled and grated
1 raw beetroot, peeled and grated
1 tablespoon ground fenugreek
1 tablespoon paprika
2 teaspoons ground coriander
2 teaspoons turmeric
2 teaspoons mixed herbs
2 teaspoons sugar
2 teaspoons salt
2 teaspoons cracked
  black pepper
2 corn on cobs, kernels
  sliced off (or 175g tinned corn)
40g basil, stalks removed,
  leaves chopped
juice and zest of 3 limes
400g oats
300ml vegetable oil
  for shallow frying

blend until you have a smooth paste.

Put the remaining tablespoon of olive oil in a frying pan over a medium heat. Throw in your onions and lightly sauté until they are soft and translucent, then add the garlic chilli paste and cook for another five minutes. Add your grated carrot, sweet potato and beetroot into the pot with the lentils and rice, turn the heat down to medium-low and cook for another five to ten minutes, stirring, until the veg have softened. Stir in the fried onions and the drained black beans, then add the ground fenugreek, paprika, coriander, turmeric, mixed herbs, sugar, salt and black pepper. Cook (still on a medium-low heat) for another five minutes, then tip the whole lot into a large bowl.

Add the sweet-corn kernels, basil, lime juice and zest and the leaves of the remaining coriander. Mix through until everything is fully incorporated. Add the oats and keep mixing until you have a thick burger mix. Split it into 12 even pieces, then mould and squeeze each one between your hands to make burger shapes. You can now either cook them, or individually wrap them in clingfilm for freezing.

To cook, put the vegetable oil into a large frying pan over a medium-high heat. Test to see if the oil is hot enough by breaking a wee piece of a burger off and dropping it in the oil – if it bubbles, it is ready to cook with. Slide the burgers into the pan (carefully, to avoid hot oil splashes) and cook for four to five minutes on each side until golden brown and hot through. If you don't fancy frying them you could just bake them in an oven preheated to 190°C (170° fan) for 12 to 15 minutes. We serve the burgers with sour cream, salad and a fresh tomato salsa.

An epic winter feast of meaty goodness! We feed hoards of winter mountaineers and walkers this dish every winter at our evening winter safety mountaineering talks.

· To make this wheat and gluten free, simply replace the flour with a free-from flour and use a gluten and wheat free beer.

· Everyone has their favourite sides to go with stew – we like creamy mash and buttered green beans.

· You could add some baby potatoes to the stew roughly 40 minutes before it's ready, if you want to save on washing up.

· This freezes really well and will keep in the fridge for four days – just let it cool first. Reheat in a pan over a medium heat or in a microwave.

Beef, Chorizo and Mushroom Stew

Serves 4–6

80g plain flour

1 teaspoon dried mixed herbs

2 teaspoons paprika

1 tablespoon chopped parsley

800g butcher's stewing steak,
trimmed and diced into
3cm cubes

100ml olive oil

1 onion, diced into 2.5cm chunks

1 carrot, diced into 2.5cm chunks

200g mushrooms, thickly sliced

150g chorizo, skinned and
diced into 2.5cm chunks

2 bay leaves

2 sprigs thyme, stalks removed,
leaves roughly chopped

2 garlic cloves, roughly chopped

500ml good quality beer
(we use Cairngorm Stag Ale
or Black Gold)

150ml hot water

1 tablespoon tomato paste

1 tablespoon sugar

salt

cracked black pepper

Combine the flour, mixed herbs, paprika and chopped parsley in a large bowl; using a spoon mix them together. Add the beef and toss in the flour mix with your hands so all the pieces are evenly coated.

Put 50ml of the oil in a large, heavy-bottomed stock or soup pot on a medium-high heat. Add the onions, carrots, mushrooms, chorizo, bay leaves, thyme and garlic and sauté until the onions are translucent and the chorizo has released its oil. Remove the pot from the heat and scrape out the contents onto a plate using a slotted spoon. Place the pot back on the heat and add the remaining 50ml olive oil. When the pan and oil are hot again, add the floured beef (discarding any flour left in the bowl). Stir constantly to prevent the meat from sticking. Once the beef is starting to brown, add the fried vegetables and chorizo back to the pot and give it a good stir. Pour over the beer and hot water and stir through to mix, then bring up to a gentle simmer and cook for 2 to 2½ hours, uncovered, stirring occasionally.

When the meat is tender and the sauce is thick and glossy, stir in the tomato paste and sugar and season to taste. Simmer for a further three to four minutes and serve.

Take a simple spud, bake it, scoop out the centre, mash it, add your fillings and seasoning, put it back in the skin and you have an all-singing, all-dancing baked potato.

- Use either salted or unsalted butter – just season to taste after you have mashed the butter through the potatoes.

- If you can't find smoked chicken, use a good quality ham or some cooked streaky bacon.

- If mango is a bit too adventurous for you, try tinned pineapple. In fact you can use any flavours you want: I really like chorizo, red pepper, paprika and basil.

- This is just as good made with baked sweet potatoes: you will just need to handle them gently as the skins are not as robust as potatoes.

Smoked Chicken, Mango and Spring Onion Stuffed Baked Spuds

Serves 4

for the spuds:

4 large baking spuds
   (about 10 x 7cm each),
   scrubbed clean
a drizzle of olive oil

for the filling:

30g butter

40ml double cream

140g mango, peeled and diced

150g smoked chicken,
   roughly shredded

2 spring onions, finely chopped

100g Cheddar, grated

salt

cracked black pepper

Preheat your oven to 200ºC (180ºC fan). Place the potatoes on a baking tray and rub a little olive oil into their skins. Season with some salt and black pepper and bake for about 60 to 75 minutes. Gently push a sharp knife into the middle of the potato to see if they are done: if it goes in easy they are cooked. As soon as they are ready, take them out of the oven and cut a thin lid off the top with a sharp knife. Turn your oven down to 180ºC (160ºC fan). Use a clean tea towel to hold the potato and scoop the flesh out with a spoon into a mixing bowl until you're left with an empty potato skin (leave a thin layer of potato in the skin to help support it). Place the empty skins back on the baking tray.

Add the butter and cream to the potato in the bowl and mash until you have sexy mashed potato. Add the mango, chicken, spring onion and half of the Cheddar. Stir through and taste, then add salt and black pepper until you have a flavour you are happy with. Spoon the filling back into the skins, piling the mash up nice and high. Sprinkle the remaining grated Cheddar over the top and pop back in the oven for 15 to 20 minutes, until they are hot and golden brown.

On a trip back home, I was invited to a friend's for dinner but was told to bring something for the barbecue. Gulp... I felt hugely under pressure having left the area and become a chef who was written about by the local press for my cooking achievements – I could hardly rock up with a packet of sausages. So I nipped to the shops, raided Nana's herb patch and came up with this recipe. It went down a treat and when I got back to the café it went on the menu.

- To get the best flavour, marinate for 24 hours if possible. The chicken will keep for up to three days in the marinade in the fridge.

- This is also a great marinade for pork. Don't leave it in for longer than six hours, as the meat starts to go mushy.

- If you're cooking over an open flame on the barbecue, make sure you drain the chicken well or you'll get some big flames.

- The cooked chicken works really well in a salad with blue cheese, crisp apple slices, walnuts and a really tart dressing. To serve this way, I'd slice each chicken breast into four long slices before it goes in the marinade.

Cider and Sage BBQ Chicken

Serves 4

---

4 chicken breasts
100ml pear cider
100ml apple juice
70ml olive oil, plus a little for frying
12 sage leaves, chopped
1 red chilli, finely diced (keep the seeds in if you like a kick)
1 teaspoon salt
½ teaspoon cracked black pepper

Trim your chicken, removing all traces of bone, skin and fat. Slice each breast into two lengthwise to help get the flavour into the middle of the breast. Place the chicken pieces in a large plastic tub and cover with cider, apple juice, olive oil, sage, chilli, salt and cracked black pepper. Stir everything through, cover and put in the fridge. Marinate for a minimum of 12 hours, preferably 24.

Lightly oil a large frying pan and put over a medium heat or fire up your barbecue. Cook the chicken for about five to eight minutes on each side until golden brown and cooked through.

My favourite winter or post-exercise feast! I think this one tastes even better the next day, reheated and served with a big spoon of whatever relish or chutney you like alongside.

· If you are gluten or wheat free, just use free-from pasta and flour.

· Try using whatever cheese you like instead of Cheddar; Gruyère is really nice.

· Go nice and slowly with your sauce – getting this right will give you a top-notch mac'n' cheese. However, if your

cheese sauce does go lumpy, use a stick blender to smooth it out.

· You don't have to use macaroni – I like big, chunky pasta shells.

· This will keep in the fridge for up to four days. Reheat it in the microwave as the oven tends to dry it out.

Posh Mac 'n' Cheese

Serves 6

for the pasta:
250g dry pasta
1 tablespoon butter
300g smoked streaky bacon,
  chopped
1 large leek, finely sliced
1 large onion, chopped
1 medium red pepper,
  roughly chopped
100g cherry tomatoes, halved
100g mature Cheddar cheese,
  grated
50g spinach, sliced
3 tablespoons chopped
  flat-leaf parsley
1 teaspoon paprika
cracked black pepper

for the cheese sauce:
80g butter
80g plain flour
600ml full fat milk
½ teaspoon Dijon mustard
100g mature Cheddar cheese,
  grated
salt
cracked black pepper

for the topping:
5 tablespoons finely
  grated Parmesan
5 tablespoons fresh
  breadcrumbs

30 x 23cm casserole dish

Preheat your oven to 190°C (170°C fan).

Bring a large pan of salted water to the boil, then add your pasta and cook until just done. Drain and refresh in cold water, then drain again and put in a large mixing bowl.

Melt the butter in a frying pan over a medium heat, then add your bacon, leek and onion and fry until the onions are soft and translucent. Add to the cooked pasta along with the red pepper, cherry tomatoes, grated Cheddar, spinach, flat-leaf parsley and paprika. Give it a good grind of black pepper and stir everything together so it is well mixed.

Make your sauce: melt the butter in a heavy-bottomed saucepan over a medium heat. When the butter is foaming, add your flour and stir with a wooden spoon to make a smooth roux. Cook, stirring, until the roux starts to bubble – don't let it get too brown. Keep stirring and slowly add the milk, little by little, until it is all mixed in and you have no lumps. Still stirring, bring the sauce up to a simmer and let it gently cook for five to ten minutes until it is thick and smooth and no longer tastes floury. Take off the heat. Stir in the Dijon mustard and grated Cheddar and season to taste.

Pour the cheese sauce into the pasta vegetable mix and stir it through so everything is combined. Tip into your casserole dish and sprinkle with the Parmesan and breadcrumbs. Bake for about 30 minutes until golden brown and hot.

Mum definitely inherited her dad's passion for food and cooking, but this recipe was one I hated as a kid. She used to use the whole chicken and cook it till the meat fell off the bone; the problem was she made it all the time. I had forgotten all about it until one day she Facebooked me a picture of the dreaded chicken pie and I thought 'I am going to take that recipe, pimp it up and make it a special at the café'. So this started as Mum's recipe but has now evolved to a recipe I can eat again!

· To make this gluten or wheat free, use free-from bread to make the breadcrumbs and check the ingredients of your wholegrain mustard.

· I know 187ml white wine seems like a random measurement, but it's the size of those individual wee bottles you can buy so you don't have to open a big bottle if you don't want to.

· Mum likes to add some streaky bacon when she's sautéing the onions – it's good either way.

· This will keep in the fridge for four days – reheat it in the microwave to prevent it drying out.

Mum's Chicken Pie

Serves 6

for the chicken:

450g skinless chicken breasts
  or thighs
400ml full fat milk
100ml water
3 bay leaves
10 peppercorns
4 sprigs thyme
3 garlic cloves, peeled and
  left whole
1 white onion, roughly diced
1 small leek, finely sliced
1 small carrot, grated
1 stick celery, finely sliced

for the sauce:

1 teaspoon olive oil
1 white onion, thinly sliced
2 sprigs thyme, stalks removed
187ml white wine
600ml double cream
1 teaspoon wholegrain mustard

for the crumble top:

250g fresh wholemeal
  breadcrumbs
60g pumpkin seeds
60g dried apricots, chopped
zest of 1 orange
8 sage leaves, finely chopped
90g butter, melted
cracked black pepper

25cm round casserole dish
  or roasting tray

Place your chicken pieces in a heavy-bottomed pan that fits them snugly, then pour over the milk and water. Add the bay leaves, peppercorns, thyme sprigs, garlic and onion. Bring up to a simmer on a medium heat and leave to gently cook for about 30 minutes, until the chicken is very tender and starting to fall apart.

While the chicken is cooking, preheat your oven to 180°C (160°C fan) and then get on with the sauce. Heat the oil in a large saucepan, then add the onion and thyme and sauté over a medium heat until the onions are soft and translucent. Pour in the white wine, turn up to a high heat and bring to a rolling boil.

Reduce the wine by half, then add the double cream and again bring up to a boil and reduce by half (you may need to turn the heat down a little to stop the cream boiling over). Stir in the wholegrain mustard.

Put your leeks, carrot and celery into a large bowl. Drain the cooked chicken and, when it's cool enough to handle, shred it into the bowl with the vegetables. Pour the sauce over the top, season, then stir to combine. Scrape the filling into your dish.

Put the breadcrumbs into a bowl and add the pumpkin seeds, dried apricots, orange zest, sage, melted butter and plenty of cracked black pepper. Mix it all through with your hands, squeezing and rubbing between your fingers to make a crumble. Sprinkle the crumble over the chicken/vegetable filling and bake for 30 minutes until hot in the middle and golden brown and crispy on top.

This recipe came from the legend that is our jolly boy John! John was with us for a season, a Skye boy, amazing chef and totally lovely bloke. He served this tartiflette recipe to hungry skiers while cooking in the Alps – it's a cracker and you'll find it on our menu every winter.

· Making a veggie version? Hold back on the bacon and add some raw spinach along with some walnuts. Delish!

· Use good quality potatoes (Maris Piper work well) and make sure they are all about the same size so they take the same amount of time to cook.

· Be quite generous with the salt and pepper when you're cooking the potatoes – put about a teaspoon of salt and a teaspoon of cracked black pepper into the water you're cooking them in.

· Don't overcook the potatoes – they should be about three-quarters cooked and still a little hard in the middle or they will turn to mush by the time they are cool enough to slice.

· You can make this up in advance and keep it in the fridge until you are ready to eat – it will keep for four days uncooked. I would add the cheese and double cream just before putting in the oven. It will take a little longer in the oven if you're cooking it from the fridge.

Tartiflette

Serves 4–6

1kg potatoes, peeled but
  left whole
2 tablespoons olive oil
250g onions, thinly sliced
2 large garlic cloves,
  crushed or grated
250g streaky smoked bacon,
  sliced into strips
4 tablespoons chopped
  fresh parsley
220g Reblochon cheese
  (or a good quality Brie),
  cut into strips
330ml double cream
salt
cracked black pepper

30 x 23cm baking dish

Place the potatoes in a pan of water seasoned with some salt and black pepper. Bring to the boil and cook until the potatoes are nearly done but still a little bit hard in the middle – they will continue to cook while they are cooling. Drain and leave to cool.

Put the oil in a frying pan and add the onions, garlic and bacon. Lightly sauté till all is lightly cooked but not coloured. Preheat your oven to 190°C (170°C fan).

When the potatoes are cool enough to handle, cut into slices about a centimetre thick. Put them in a bowl with the bacon mixture (including any juices from the pan), the parsley, a teaspoon of salt and two teaspoons of cracked black pepper and gently mix together. Scrape into your baking dish (sometimes I use six individual dishes) and smooth down. Cover with the strips of Reblochon, then pour over the cream. Bake for 30 to 40 minutes, until golden brown and bubbling. Serve with the Waldorf salad on page 87, some chunky bread and (essential) a glass of cold, crisp white wine.

Roots

My grandparents were a huge inspiration and support to me growing up and have been instrumental in my passion for good food and cooking. Their life stories have influenced mine in many ways.

GRANDDAD

Hans Sauer (who became John Saver) was born in Brennberg, Hungary, close to the Austrian border. His mother was a teenager when he was born, who had got pregnant when she was raped by a Russian soldier. He never knew this – his family told him he was fathered by a man who had died in a mine – and she completely doted on him. She went on to marry and have three more children, and when the Soviets took over their village she was thrown out of her house and given a tiny, one-bedroomed annexe with no running water to live in with her four children.

When Granddad was 18, he was almost caught helping to smuggle people from his village out of Soviet-controlled Hungary into the West. The friend he was with was shot and killed and Granddad knew he had to run to escape the same fate. So run he did, across the border to Austria. He spent two years living in an uncle's basement and, when that became too risky, travelled by night to Belgium and somehow made his way to England and boarded a boat to Australia. He taught himself English and many other languages along the way.

When Granddad arrived in Australia he worked on a sugar cane farm, living in shed-like accommodation with other immigrants. He worked hard, he saved and he educated himself as he went. He loved his new life: he bought himself a snazzy soft-top car and some dress suits, and discovered a love of opera and classical music. He was living a life he could have never had in Hungary.

NANA

My nana, Heather, was born in Southland, New Zealand to Nellie Hibbs and her saw-miller husband, Bill. Nellie has to have been one of the hardest working ladies in Southland: she and Bill bought a huge piece of bush in the country and they set about clearing it with a single bulldozer and by hand. Nana told fabulous tales of camping out in the bush for the night with her brother, Keith, hunting and cooking dinner over fires. They had very little money so Nana would hunt possums, clean their skins up and sell them for a little extra cash.

Nellie and Bill built their own house, cutting the piles which the house sat upon from huge totara trees. It was a hard and heavy life, but they all thrived. Nellie made their clothes, milked the cows, killed for their meat and cooked everything from scratch. Washing was all done by hand and horses were used to turn the land over. The children would walk six miles to school every day, whatever the weather. Nana was very clever and was always independent, stubborn and free spirited, so I guess it came as no surprise when she told her parents that she wanted to become a doctor. They scraped enough money together to get her into a nursing college and once she qualified as a nurse, she saved enough to get to Sydney, Australia to work... Little did she know she was about to be swept off her feet by a foreign man, much to her mother's horror!

Nana and Granddad's stories of meeting were quite different; I like to imagine their eyes meeting over a hospital bed and that was it. However, knowing my nana, I am sure it couldn't have been that easy – I bet she played a hard game of chase. In the short of it, they fell in love and married and after a few years moved back to New Zealand, where they lived on a farm and brought up my mum and her brother, Willie. My mum speaks fondly of this time: she was a daddy's girl and her memories are of Nana coming home to find the house a riot, with happy kids and no money to pay the bills as Granddad had spent it all on salamis, livers, fine cuts of meat and baking ingredients.

POSTSCRIPT

In 1982, my granddad returned to Hungary to see his mother for the first time since he escaped. He returned three more times before he died and in 1986 he took my nana with him to meet his mother and siblings, nephews and cousins. This was a very special time: we really felt this foreign, extended family were a little closer to us (and when I arrived in Europe, one of my first ports of call was Vienna, where they now all live). Knowing them helped us understand Granddad better – this carefree, fun, food-obsessed creature. He died when I was 13 and the main thing I remember from that day was opening the cupboard to find a huge pile of pancakes he had cooked that morning.

We shall be donating 10 pence
from every Afgan Biscuit,
Ginger Crunch & Flat White Sold
towards the Christchurch
EarthQuake appeal.
Thank You for your Help!

NZ
arth Quake
Relief
Fund

Baking

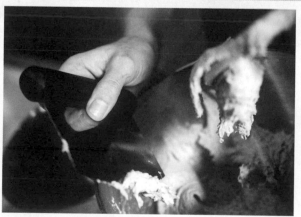

Baking

NO CAKE MIXER?
Just use elbow grease and zip up your man suit... Nah, there are loads of alternatives to posh cake mixers. You can go back to old-school hand beating with a whisk or hand beater: it will take a lot longer, but you will get the same result eventually. If you're mixing the old-school way, soften your butter a little in the microwave to make it a bit easier. You will just need to be more patient. Most people will have a hand-held electric mixer and these do a grand job. We always use one for whipped cream, as you get a better result than in a free-standing cake mixer. You are also less likely to over-beat with a hand-held mixer, but they will take a little longer and the annoying thing is you have to stand there holding it! But there are pros and cons to everything.

HAND MIXING
When I make any cakes that start with creamed butter and sugar and the eggs added one by one, I literally use my hand to fold in the dry ingredients. My theory is that, doing it this way, you are less likely to over-mix because you have the larger surface area on your hand than on a small wooden spoon – it works for me!

BAKING FOR PEOPLE WITH DIETARY REQUIREMENTS
We use Dove's gluten free flour in all our dietary cakes.

We add xanthan gum to replace the elasticity that gluten naturally provides in wheat flour.

Make sure you check your baking powder is gluten free as lots of them are bulked up with wheat flour.

If you are cooking for a friend that has gluten and/or wheat intolerances, you will need to clean out your oven. We hose our ovens out before baking any gluten/wheat free cakes. It's amazing how much flour gets into the fan when you bake. Make sure you don't cross-contaminate ingredients, utensils and surfaces.

BUTTER
We use salted butter unless specified; we rarely add salt to our cakes, as the salt is already in the butter. Always use butter when listed, not inferior substitutes.

VANILLA
Pick a top-notch vanilla paste or extract for the best flavour – you will notice a huge difference if you have been using vanilla essence up to now. Remember to make a tub of vanilla sugar with any leftover vanilla pods (page 293).

BUTTERMILK
If you can't get hold of buttermilk, use a full fat natural yogurt as a replacement.

SUGAR
We use caster sugar rather than granulated sugar for everything in our kitchen. It has a smaller crystal so makes a lighter cake and melts quicker when making caramel sauce and jams.

EGGS

We always use large free-range eggs; you see such a difference in your baking and cooking with these. No battery or barn egg has ever crossed the Mountain Café delivery door! We store eggs at room temperature, not in the fridge.

CHOCOLATE

We buy our chocolate from an amazing chocolate supplier in England and have it couriered up weekly. Wherever you get yours, avoid cheap, fatty chocolate and get your hands on as high a grade as you can afford – for baking I recommend at least 50% cocoa solids for dark and 30% for white.

ADDING EGGS TO MELTED RECIPES

In some of our recipes (like the Chocolate Beetroot Cake on page 171 or Whisky Cake on page 188) you add the eggs to a pan of melted ingredients. Make sure you check the temperature of the mix before you add the eggs – you need to be able to hold your finger in it. If you can't, it's too hot and the eggs will scramble. We once had some perfectly cooked egg in the middle of our Chocolate Beetroot Cake because someone rushed the prep – never a good look...

MELTING CHOCOLATE

We don't use bain-maries or fancy chocolate melting dishes to avoid getting water or steam into the melting chocolate. Water/ steam is death to chocolate and will make it seize up so always be super careful to avoid any excessive moisture getting anywhere near the pan when you're melting chocolate or making ganache. We use a heavy-bottomed pan placed over the lowest possible temperature on the hob, and we keep stirring once the chocolate starts to melt. Remove the pan from the heat just before the chocolate is fully melted and continue to stir until it is smooth and glossy. If you overheat the chocolate (you'll know because it will lack shine and stick heavily to the pan), you can add a small handful of grated chocolate and stir it in off the heat. This should stop the chocolate from getting that strange white coating when it sets.

CAKE TINS

We line the bottom of all our cake tins with baking paper to make it easier to get the cakes out. We use sunflower spread to grease our tins and are very generous with our greasing. I would also recommend wrapping the outside/bottom of springform tins with tin foil to stop any cake batter from escaping and dripping into the oven. No one likes cleaning their oven!

FREEZING CAKES

Most of the cakes in this section will freeze, un-iced. Wrap them in clingfilm before you put them in the freezer, then unwrap before you defrost on a wire rack to prevent the cake going soggy.

CUTTING SLICES OR CAKES

When cutting fridge slices, millionaire's shortbread and brownies, heat a knife in a jug of boiling hot water. Quickly wipe dry to remove the water and cut the slice with the hot knife, repeating the process as you go. This gives a nice clean finish with tidy edges.

An epic summer cake that is perfect for afternoon tea with bubbly wine and fresh blueberries.

· Store the cake at room temperature in an airtight container. It will keep for four to five days.

· This freezes well, wrapped up in some clingfilm. Unwrap and put on a rack to defrost to stop it going soggy.

Blueberry, Lime and Coconut Cake

Serves 8–10

for the cake:
170g butter, softened
170g caster sugar
2 large eggs
170g self-raising flour, sieved
140g fresh blueberries
30g desiccated coconut,
   plus a little for the top
juice and zest of 1 lime

for the syrup:
juice of 2 limes, zest of 1
60g caster sugar

20cm springform cake tin

Grease your tin and preheat your oven to 170°C (150°C fan). Cream the butter and sugar together until fluffy and pale – either by hand or using a mixer with the balloon whisk attachment. Even with a mixer, this can take up to 15 minutes. Stop and scrape the mix off the sides of the bowl from time to time so it is all evenly mixed.

Beat in the eggs one at a time, mixing for at least two or three minutes between each one – don't add the eggs all at once or it's likely to curdle. Then add the flour, blueberries, coconut, and lime juice and zest and gently fold in using your hand. (Don't use a cake mixer to add the dry ingredients and be careful not to over-mix or you will have a heavy cake.) Scrape the batter into the prepared cake tin and bake near the bottom of the oven for 50 minutes until a skewer comes out clean.

To make the syrup, place the lime juice and zest in a small pan with the caster sugar. When the cake is about to come out of the oven, put the pan on a medium heat and gently bring to a simmer. Cook till the sugar is dissolved and the syrup is clear, but don't let it thicken or colour. Drizzle the light syrup evenly over the hot cake and sprinkle with a little bit more desiccated coconut. Leave to cool in the tin on a rack.

The sweetness of carrot and the earthiness of the zucchini is a winning combination and makes a moist, high fibre cake that can be dairy free if you leave off the lemon frosting.

· This keeps for four days in an airtight container at room temperature. Don't refrigerate (it makes the sponge stale).

· You can freeze the cake without the frosting; wrap it in clingfilm to freeze and unwrap to defrost on a cooling rack to prevent it going soggy.

Carrot and Zucchini Cake

Serves 8–10

for the cake:
210ml good quality vegetable oil
2 large eggs
175g dark brown sugar
100g zucchini (courgette), grated
120g carrot, peeled and grated
300g wholemeal flour
1½ teaspoons baking powder
1½ teaspoons bicarbonate
   of soda
1½ teaspoons mixed spice
2½ tablespoons poppy seeds,
   plus more for the top

for the lemon frosting:
170g cream cheese
260g icing sugar
60g butter, melted
zest of 1 lemon

20cm springform cake tin

Preheat the oven to 170°C (150°C fan). Grease your cake tin.

Put the oil, eggs and sugar in a bowl (or in a cake mixer) and beat together until smooth, glossy and lighter in colour. Add the grated zucchini and carrot, wholemeal flour, baking powder, bicarbonate of soda, mixed spice and poppy seeds and gently mix until fully incorporated. Scrape the batter into your prepared tin and bake near the bottom of the oven for about 60 minutes until a skewer comes out clean. Leave the cake to cool in the tin on a rack.

Once the cake is completely cold, remove it from the tin and put it on a plate or serving board. Using a serrated knife, cut the cake horizontally through the middle to get two layers.

Put the cream cheese in a bowl and add the icing sugar, melted butter and lemon zest. Gently mix everything together (on a low speed if you're using an electric mixer), then beat more firmly till you have a glossy, smooth frosting. Spread half of the frosting onto the bottom layer leaving a gap of about 3cm around the edge of the cake, then place the second layer on top. Press gently but firmly down to stick the layers together, then spread the remaining frosting over the top of the cake. Sprinkle with poppy seeds as a garnish.

This was my mum's recipe which I stole and then added beetroot to. Us Kiwis go mad for beetroot! I came up with this 15 years ago when my old head chef asked me to make a cake for her to take to a radio interview about cheffing in London. I thought, 'This should be fun, let's Kiwi this up...' They were speechless that someone would put beetroot in a cake and that it tasted good!

· Don't open the oven door for at least 40 minutes after the cake goes in the oven or it might sink in the middle. When you check to see if the cake's ready, use a skewer and slant it in from the edge to the middle (don't just poke it straight down in the middle of the cake) – this also helps prevent sinking.

· When the cake has cooled but is still a little bit warm, cover the tin with clingfilm until it's completely cold to get a lovely, moist texture.

· Store at room temperature in an airtight container for up to four days. You can freeze it too: we have a regular customer who wraps it up in clingfilm and freezes the cake, frosting and all.

Chocolate Beetroot Cake

Serves 8–10

for the cake:

150g good quality
   dark chocolate chips
100g butter, diced
170ml hot water
120g cooked beetroot, grated
200g caster sugar
2 large eggs
1½ teaspoons vanilla extract
125g self-raising flour
110g plain flour
⅔ teaspoon baking powder
¾ teaspoon bicarbonate of soda
35g cocoa powder

for the vanilla frosting:

170g cream cheese
260g icing sugar
60g butter, melted
1 vanilla pod, halved lengthwise
   and pulp scraped out
melted chocolate and/or
   Maltesers for garnish

20cm springform cake tin

Grease your tin and preheat the oven to 170°C (150°C fan).

Put the chocolate, butter, hot water and grated beetroot into a heavy-bottomed pan that's large enough to take all the ingredients. Place on a low heat, stirring occasionally, until the chocolate and butter are melted. Let the mix cool until you can hold a finger in it, then whisk in the sugar, eggs and vanilla till everything is glossy and smooth.

Sieve the flours, baking powder, bicarbonate of soda and cocoa powder into the pan and whisk again to get a smooth batter – you can't over-beat this one so make sure it's really thoroughly mixed with no lumps. Scrape the batter into your prepared cake tin and bake near the bottom of the oven for 50 to 60 minutes, until a skewer comes out clean. Leave to cool in the tin on a rack.

Once the cake is completely cold, remove from the tin and place on a plate or serving board. Place the cream cheese, icing sugar, melted butter and vanilla pulp into a bowl and gently mix together either with a mixer or by hand. Once everything is incorporated, beat faster till the frosting is glossy and smooth. Spread the frosting onto the top and sides of the cake, then drizzle with melted chocolate or scatter on Maltesers as a garnish.

What more can you want in life? Coffee in a cake, with creamy coffee frosting – personally I would have a slice with a strong flat white, job done!

· Don't worry if the mix splits when you add the eggs, sometimes it does! Just keep on mixing – it will not affect the end product.

· The cake will keep for four days in an airtight tin at room temperature. Don't refrigerate as it makes the sponge stale.

Coffee Cake

Serves 8–10

for the cake:

1 heaped tablespoon
  instant coffee granules

2½ tablespoons boiling water

300g butter, softened

300g caster sugar

4 large eggs

300g self-raising flour

for the coffee frosting:

1½ tablespoons boiling water

1 tablespoon instant coffee
  granules

200g cream cheese

75g butter, melted

400g icing sugar

2 x 20cm spring form cake tins

Grease your tins and preheat your oven to 170°C (150°C fan).

Add the coffee granules to the boiling water in a small bowl and stir to dissolve. Pour the coffee into a large mixing bowl with the butter and sugar and cream until fluffy and pale – if you're using a cake mixer, use the balloon whisk attachment and stop occasionally to scrape the mix off the sides of the bowl so it's all evenly mixed. Add the eggs one at a time, giving at least two to three minutes mixing between each egg – don't add the eggs all at once! Then add the flour and fold in by hand. Be careful not to over-mix, and don't mix the flour in with a cake mixer or you will have a flat and heavy cake. Divide the batter between the cake tins and bake near the bottom of the oven for 40 minutes until a skewer comes out clean. Leave the cakes to cool in their tins on a rack.

Once cakes are completely cold, remove from the tins and place one on your plate or serving board. To make the frosting, add the boiling water to the coffee granules in a small bowl and stir till dissolved. Put the cream cheese in a mixing bowl with the melted butter and icing sugar and add the coffee.

Beat until everything is combined and you have a smooth, glossy, fluffy frosting. Evenly spread about a third of the frosting onto the cake on the plate, leaving a gap of about 3cm around the edge. Place the second cake on top, pressing gently but firmly down to stick the layers together. Cover the top and sides with the remaining icing – we decorate it with chocolate-coated coffee beans.

This recipe is a family treasure. My granddad was an amazing baker but, in the seventies and eighties, men in New Zealand that baked were viewed as a bit odd (to be polite). I think Granddad felt that he would be named and shamed if he was ever found out, so he had a rule: if anyone asked, Nana baked it. And so his home baking was kept secret and he threatened that if anyone found out he would never bake again. We never let on to anyone... It's odd, looking back, to think about Granddad baking while Nana tended to the farm and animals, but that's the way they were, different in all the best ways.

· Try serving this warm with a little caramel sauce (page 46) as a pudding.

· This will keep for five days in an airtight container at room temperature. It also freezes really well, wrapped up in clingfilm.

Granddad's Date Loaf

(DF)

Serves 8

160g pitted dates, chopped

100g dairy free margarine
  (we use Pure sunflower spread)

2 teaspoons bicarbonate of soda

250ml boiling water

1 large egg

175g dark brown sugar

100g walnut pieces

2 teaspoons vanilla extract

225g plain flour

2 teaspoons baking powder

23 x 13cm loaf tin

Place the dates, margarine, bicarbonate of soda and boiling water in a large metal bowl. Set aside for an hour to let the dates soften.

Preheat your oven to 170°C (150°C fan). Grease and lightly flour your loaf tin. Add the egg, dark brown sugar, walnut pieces and vanilla extract to the softened date mix. Beat really well until the egg and sugar are fully incorporated. Sieve the flour and baking powder into the bowl of wet ingredients and gently but thoroughly fold through. Pour the batter into your greased tin and bake for 55 minutes, until a skewer comes out clean. Leave to cool in the loaf tin on a rack.

Serve with lashings of butter.

We have a customer who orders this cake four or five times a year. She calls it the ugly cake – she has it with no frosting and I guess it is a bit ugly on its own. It's her secret naughty pleasure – she is 99% vegan but this is her one weakness. She just can't give up the ugly cake...

· If you're using frozen raspberries, you can just put them straight into the batter. Don't worry about defrosting them first.

· This will keep for four days in an airtight container, kept at room temperature.

Hummingbird Cake

Serves 8–10

for the cake:
225g caster sugar
2 eggs
225ml vegetable oil
2 medium bananas
⅔ teaspoon cinnamon
⅔ teaspoon vanilla extract
225g plain flour
⅔ teaspoon bicarbonate of soda
75g tinned chopped pineapple, drained
80g frozen or fresh raspberries, plus some for the top
70g pecan nuts, plus some for the top

for the lemon frosting:
250g cream cheese
390g icing sugar
90g butter, melted
juice and zest of 1 lemon

2 x 20cm springform cake tins

Preheat the oven to 170°C (150°C fan) and grease your cake tins. Put the sugar, eggs, oil, banana, cinnamon and vanilla extract in a large bowl and beat with a mixer on high speed until smooth, lump-free and glossy. Sieve the flour and bicarbonate of soda together, then add to the bowl along with the pineapple, raspberries and pecans. Mix on a low speed until fully incorporated – you can do all this by hand, but it is more labour-intensive. Divide the batter between the two prepared tins and bake near the bottom of the oven for about 30 minutes, until a skewer comes out clean. If the cake starts to go too dark on the top while it's cooking, place a piece of tin foil over the top towards the end. Leave the cakes to cool in their tins on a rack.

Once the cakes are completely cold remove both from the tins and place one on a plate or serving board. To make the frosting, put the cream cheese, icing sugar, melted butter and lemon juice and zest into a mixing bowl and gently mix together. Once everything is incorporated, beat it more firmly till you have a glossy and smooth frosting. Spread half the frosting onto the cake on the plate leaving a gap of about 3cm around the edge, then place the second cake on top, pressing gently but firmly down to stick the layers together. Cover the top of the cake with the remaining frosting and, if you like, decorate with raspberries, banana chips and pecan nuts.

There is not much to say here except lemony, buttery, deliciousness...

· Be particularly careful not to over-mix this one when you add the dry ingredients – use your hand and go gently.

· You can turn this into an orange cake by using one orange instead of the lemons.

If I make it into an orange cake, I add two tablespoons of poppy seeds to the batter and use orange juice for the drizzle.

· This will keep for up to five days in an airtight tin at room temperature.

Lemon Loaf

Serves 8

---

for the cake:

200g butter, softened

200g caster sugar

zest of 2 lemons

2 large eggs

110ml full fat milk

200g self-raising flour

1½ teaspoons baking powder

for the drizzle:

juice of 3 lemons (about 90ml)

90g caster sugar

23 x 13cm loaf tin

Grease and line your tin with greaseproof paper. Preheat your oven to 170°C (150°C fan).

Cream the butter, sugar and lemon zest together in a large bowl until fluffy and pale – use the balloon whisk attachment if you are using a mixer and stop occasionally to scrape the mix off the sides of the bowl so it is evenly mixed. This can take up to 15 minutes to get it really fluffy, even using an electric mixer. Add the eggs one at a time, mixing for at least two to three minutes between each egg. Beat in the milk – it will look curdled but that's ok, just keep on beating and it will get past this point. Once the milk is fully incorporated, sieve the flour and baking powder over the wet ingredients and gently fold them in using your hand or a wooden spoon to get a thick, smooth cake batter. Scrape the batter into your prepared loaf tin and bake near the bottom of the oven for 60 minutes, until a skewer comes out clean. Be careful only to test it with a skewer when the top of the loaf no longer wobbles or it will flop in the middle.

Put the lemon juice and caster sugar into a small pan. When the cake is ready to take out of the oven, put the syrup pan on a medium heat and gently bring to a simmer. Cook till the sugar is dissolved and the syrup is clear, but don't let it thicken or colour. Drizzle the syrup evenly over the hot loaf and leave it to cool in the tin on a rack.

An American-style, lightly chocolatey sponge with lashings of cream cheese frosting; this is a stunning cake that looks super duper and tastes incredible for all occasions.

· If you can't get buttermilk, use full fat natural yogurt instead.

· It really is important to sieve the flour, baking powder and cocoa together four times to get a nice light cake with an even rise.

· Make sure you mix the red food colouring in really well so you don't end up with a streaky cake.

· This will keep for four days in an airtight tin at room temperature. Don't put it in the fridge or the sponge will go stale.

Red Velvet Cake

Serves 8–10

for the cake:
225g plain flour
¼ teaspoon baking powder
15g cocoa powder
225g caster sugar
2 eggs
⅔ teaspoon salt
⅔ teaspoon vanilla extract
250ml vegetable oil
150ml buttermilk
1½ teaspoons bicarbonate
   of soda
25ml red wine vinegar
15g red food colour paste

for the vanilla frosting:
320g cream cheese
500g icing sugar
120g butter, melted
1 vanilla pod, halved lengthwise
   and pulp scraped out

20cm springform cake tin

Preheat your oven to 170°C (150°C fan). Grease the cake tin.

Sieve the flour, baking powder and cocoa powder four times. Put the sugar, eggs, salt and vanilla into a large bowl and beat until thick, pale and creamy. Still beating, pour in the oil and mix until it's fully combined.

Mix the buttermilk, bicarbonate of soda and vinegar in a bowl. Add to the egg mix along with the sieved dry ingredients and beat together until you have a smooth cake batter. Add the food colouring and mix in until the batter is a deep red with no streaks. Scrape the batter into your greased tin and bake near the bottom of the oven for about 60 to 75 minutes until a skewer comes out clean. Don't open the oven door until the cake has been in for at least 40 minutes or it might sink in the middle. Leave the cake to cool in the tin on a rack. Once the cake is completely cold, remove it from the tin and cut it into three layers with a serrated knife. Put one layer on your serving plate.

Put the cream cheese in a mixing bowl with the icing sugar, melted butter and the pulp from the vanilla pod. Mix together to get a smooth, glossy frosting. Spread a quarter of the frosting onto the bottom layer of cake, leaving a gap of about 3cm around the edge. Place the second layer of cake on top, pressing gently but firmly down to stick the layers together. Repeat with another quarter of frosting and the third layer of cake. Use the remaining icing to cover the top and sides of the cake, smoothing it out as you go. Let it set for about one hour before you serve or cut.

Serve warm from the oven with Stewed Rhubarb on page 40 and cream or ice cream for a delicious pud.

· This will keep for four to five days at room temperature in an airtight container. It also freezes really well – just wrap it up in clingfilm first. To defrost, unwrap and leave on a cooling rack so it doesn't go soggy.

· When rhubarb is out of season, apple makes a lovely alternative.

· If you are using frozen raspberries, put them straight into the batter. You don't need to defrost them first.

Rhubarb, Raspberry and Orange Cake

Serves 8–10

250g butter, softened
250g caster sugar
3 large eggs
250g self-raising flour, sieved
150g raspberries, fresh or frozen
100g rhubarb, trimmed and diced
zest of 1 orange

20cm springform cake tin

Grease your tin and preheat the oven to 170°C (150°C fan).

In a large bowl, cream the butter and sugar together until fluffy and pale, using the balloon whisk attachment if you're using a cake mixer. Stop mixing and scrape down the sides of the bowl occasionally so it is all evenly mixed. It can take up to 15 minutes to get the mix really light and fluffy.

Add the eggs one at a time, beating for at least two or three minutes between each egg – don't add the eggs all at once or the mixture will curdle. Once they are fully incorporated, add the flour, raspberries, rhubarb and orange zest and gently fold through using your hand. Don't over-mix, and don't mix in the dry ingredients with a cake mixer or you will end up with a heavy cake. Scrape the batter into your prepared cake tin and bake near the bottom of the oven for 60 minutes or until a skewer comes out clean. If you are serving it warm for pudding, let it stand for 15 to 20 minutes, then turn the cake out and serve. Otherwise, let it cool completely in the tin.

Folks that have ordered these say they are the best Christmas cakes they've ever had. Yes, it is a bit of a faff because you have to be organised and soak your fruit in advance, and then you need to lovingly feed the cakes alcohol for a couple of weeks. But trust me, you will be proud as punch when you pull this out on Christmas day; I guarantee you will never get a bought one that tastes this good. The recipe makes a huge cake – it will feed a big family and some of the neighbours, but it lasts for ages and I'm sure it won't go to waste!

· You can easily make this gluten or wheat free by replacing the flour with gluten free flour, adding four tablespoons of xanthan gum and replacing the whisky with more sherry or brandy.

· The soaker for the cake needs a minimum of ten days to soften and rehydrate the fruit before you even start making and baking. You could cut this down to four days if you gently heat it over a medium heat and then leave at room temperature to soak, but you will lose a little flavour.

· The soaker makes an awesome mince pie filling and is what we use in ours. I would probably make about a quarter of the recipe for a batch of mince pies.

· You need two weeks after baking to feed the cake with the tipple and let it mature.

· If you don't want a really boozy cake, then use half the quantity (375ml) of ginger ale instead of the cake tipple we have suggested below.

· We have kept the icing super simple to make it manageable for all home cooks. If you are a cake-decorating shark, go for the full monty!

Seriously Epic Christmas Cake

Serves 12–16

for the soaker:
250ml brandy
250ml sherry
250ml orange juice
zest of 1 orange
zest of 1 lemon

Get started on the soaker ten days before you want to make the cake. Pour the brandy, sherry and orange juice into a large bowl, then stir in the orange zest, lemon zest, currants, cranberries, sultanas, dates, crystallised ginger, glacé cherries, vanilla extract and almond essence. Leave covered in a cool, dry place like a pantry or cupboard for ten days minimum and give it a wee stir every couple of days.

250g currants

250g dried cranberries

200g sultanas

100g pitted dates, chopped

80g crystallised ginger, chopped

80g glacé cherries

2 teaspoons vanilla extract

2 teaspoons almond essence

for the cake:

200g butter

250g dark brown sugar

50g treacle

4 large eggs

570g plain flour

150g blanched whole
   or flaked almonds

2 teaspoons bicarbonate of soda

2 teaspoons cinnamon

2 teaspoons mixed spice

1 teaspoon ground ginger

for the cake tipple:

250ml whisky

250ml brandy

250ml sherry

for the icing:

150g apricot jam

2 tablespoons water

500g natural marzipan

500g white ready-to-roll icing

a little icing sugar for the worktop

vodka or boiled water

2 x 23cm cake tins

When the ten days are up, heat your oven to 160°C (140°C fan). Grease the tins and line the base and sides with greaseproof paper. Tip the soaker fruit into a sieve or colander and leave to drain but don't press down or squeeze the liquid out: you want it juicy. In the largest mixing bowl you have, cream the butter, sugar and treacle until light, fluffy and pale – this will take about 15 minutes, even with an electric mixer. Slowly add the eggs one at a time, beating for a few minutes between each egg and scraping the bowl down to make sure it's all evenly mixed. It might look a bit curdled, but don't worry.

Tip the drained soaker fruit into another mixing bowl and sieve 120g of the flour over the top. Add the almonds, then mix everything with your hands so it's all dusted with flour. Scrape this into the egg/sugar/butter mix. Sieve the remaining 450g flour into the bowl with the bicarbonate of soda, cinnamon, mixed spice and ginger and fold in using your hand until fully incorporated. Evenly divide the batter between the lined tins and smooth out the tops with the back of a spoon. Bake near the bottom of the oven for about 1½ hours, until a skewer comes out clean.

While the cakes are baking, make your tipple: pour the whisky, brandy and sherry into a jug and stir. As soon as the cakes are out of the oven, put them on a rack in their tins and evenly drizzly half of the tipple over them. Leave to cool and soak up the booze. When they are completely cold, take them out of their tins but leave the greaseproof paper on and pop them into an airtight tin. Leave to mature for at least two weeks, dampening the cakes with a light brushing of tipple three times a week.

When you are ready to put your epic masterpiece together, unwrap your cakes and discard the greaseproof paper. Put one cake on your serving plate or board, and the other on a clean worktop. Put the apricot jam in a small pan with the water and bring to the boil, then sieve it to get a smooth glaze. Brush a third of the glaze on the top of each of the cakes, keeping the remaining third for later on. Dust your worktop with some sieved icing sugar. Cut the marzipan into two equal pieces and gently knead one on the worktop to soften it. Roll it out till it is big enough to cover the top of a cake, then place it on the jam-glazed cake on the plate, gently smoothing it down so it sticks. Trim the edges with a small sharp knife. Cover the second cake in the same way. Clean your worktop down and dust with some more sieved icing sugar. Cut the block of icing into two equal pieces and roll both out as you did the marzipan. With a pastry brush, lightly brush the marzipan on both cakes with the vodka or boiled water – you just want to make it a little damp so the icing sticks. Carefully place the icing on top of the marzipan-topped cakes, gently smooth it out, then trim the edges for a neat finish. Brush the remaining third of the apricot glaze over the white icing on the cake on the plate, then put the second cake on the top to make a double layer. If you have any leftover icing, knead it again, roll out and use a cutter to make some decorations for the top. Lightly brush the undersides with vodka or boiled water to stick them on.

After all this feeding, love and attention, you will have a very scrummy Christmas cake that was not too stressful to ice! Enjoy.

This recipe originally came from my absolute favourite chef, Alison Holst. This incredible lady revolutionised Kiwi cooking in the eighties. I have tweaked her recipe very slightly, adding whisky to keep the Scots happy and an apricot glaze to pimp it up.

· This makes a really pretty Christmas cake if your family isn't into marzipan and royal icing. When we make our Christmas version, we let them mature for at least a week after baking and give them a light brushing of whisky every other day.

· The cake lasts for three weeks in an airtight container at room temperature.

· It also freezes really well. Give it another wee drink of whisky once it has defrosted.

Whisky Fruit Cake

Serves 10–12

---

for the cake:

300g mixed dried fruit

70g glacé cherries

400ml orange juice

195ml blended whisky

190g butter, diced

250g dark brown sugar

2 large eggs

470g plain flour

3 teaspoons baking powder

150g flaked almonds

for the apricot glaze:

280g apricot jam

70ml blended whisky

for the garnish:

pecans

flaked almonds

pistachios

glacé cherries

mixed peel

23cm springform cake tin

Grease your cake tin and preheat your oven to 170°C (150°C fan).

In a saucepan big enough to take all the ingredients, place your dried fruit, glacé cherries, orange juice and 120ml of the whisky. Bring to the boil on a medium-high heat, then reduce to a simmer for five minutes. Take off the heat and stir in the butter until it has melted. Leave till the mix is cool enough to hold your finger in. Add the dark brown sugar, the remaining 75ml of whisky and the eggs and beat with a wooden spoon until really smooth and glossy. Sieve your flour and baking powder over the wet mix, add the flaked almonds and stir again until everything is fully incorporated. Tip the batter into your greased tin and bake for 60 to 70 minutes until a skewer comes out clean. Leave the cake to cool in its tin on a rack.

Take the cake from the tin and put on a serving plate. You now need two medium-sized saucepans. In one of the saucepans, melt the apricot jam and the whisky over a medium heat until it is hot and runny. Sieve this into the second pan, discarding any lumps of fruit from the sieve, to get a smooth glaze. Heat the glaze again until it is hot, then brush about half of it over the top of the cake. Garnish the top with nuts and fruit as elaborately (or not) as you like. Heat the glaze up again, adding a little more whisky if it is too thick to pour, then drizzle it slowly over the top of the cake until it is well coated. Leave to cool before serving.

A very quick and simple one-pot, one-whisk cake for white chocolate lovers.

· The cake will keep for five days in an airtight container at room temperature.

· Don't put it in the fridge or the sponge will go stale.

White Chocolate, Cranberry and Almond Cake

Serves 8–10

for the cake:

160g good quality white chocolate, chopped into chunks

120g butter

200ml warm water

265g caster sugar

⅔ teaspoon almond essence

2 large eggs

140g plain flour

140g self-raising flour

⅔ teaspoon baking powder

⅔ teaspoon bicarbonate of soda

70g flaked almonds

70g ground almonds

70g dried cranberries

for the topping:

200g good quality white chocolate, chopped

70ml double cream

wee sprinkle of dried cranberries

wee sprinkle of flaked almonds

23cm springform cake tin

Preheat your oven to 170°C (150°C fan) and grease your cake tin.

In a saucepan big enough to take all of the ingredients, melt the white chocolate, butter and water over a medium-low heat. Once everything has melted into the water, take off the heat and set aside until the mix is cool enough to hold a finger in. Add the sugar, almond essence and eggs and whisk till silky smooth. Sieve in the plain and self-raising flours, the baking powder and the bicarb, then add the flaked almonds, ground almonds and cranberries. Whisk till you have a smooth batter. Scrape into your greased tin and bake for about an hour, until a skewer comes out clean – but only check the cake once it has stopped wobbling on top or it's likely to flop. If the cake starts to brown too quickly, put some tin foil over the top towards the end of the cooking time. Leave to cool in the tin.

When the cake is completely cold, make the topping. Put the white chocolate and double cream in a heavy-bottomed pan over the lowest possible heat. Keep stirring until the chocolate has melted and the icing is smooth and glossy. Pour this over the cake (still in its tin) and leave to firm up for about 30 minutes. Sprinkle some cranberries and flaked almonds over the top then leave to fully set overnight. Run a sharp, thin-bladed knife around the edge of the tin before you take the cake out.

We were given this recipe by a customer whose family members all had different allergies; this is one cake she can bake that they can all eat. We were so touched that she shared this recipe with us – it's delicious.

· This is quite a wet cake, so a skewer will come out a bit doughy even when it's fully cooked. We use a knife instead of a skewer to check it.

· This will keep for four days in an airtight container at room temperature.

Carrot, Fruit and Nut Cake

Serves 8

for the cake:
100g pitted dates, chopped
200ml boiling water
150ml vegetable oil
250g carrot, grated
zest of 1 lemon
190g dark brown sugar
1 teaspoon bicarbonate of soda
250g plain gluten free flour
3 teaspoons gluten free
  baking powder
1 teaspoon xanthan gum
1 teaspoon ground mixed spice
70g pistachio nuts
70g pecan nuts
70g flaked almonds
70g dried cranberries
70g mixed peel
70g sultanas

for the icing:
150g icing sugar
3–4 tablespoons lemon juice
23cm springform cake tin

Preheat your oven to 170°C (150°C fan) and grease your tin.

In a bowl soak your chopped dates in the boiling water and vegetable oil for at least an hour, then blitz with a stick blender or in a food processor until there are no big lumps left.

Place your grated carrot in a large bowl with the lemon zest, brown sugar, bicarbonate of soda, gluten free flour, baking powder, xanthan gum and mixed spice. Add the pistachios, pecans, almonds, cranberries, mixed peel and sultanas, then give it all a really good mix with your hands or a wooden spoon. Pour the date purée into the bowl and mix through until you have a fully incorporated, thick cake batter. Scrape it into the prepared tin and bake for 75 minutes, or until a thin-bladed knife comes out clean. If the cake starts to look really brown on top before it is ready, put a strip of tin foil over the top

Let the cake cool in the tin on a rack. When it is completely cold, take it out of the tin and put on a serving plate. In a small bowl, mix your icing sugar and lemon juice to make a smooth, slightly runny icing. Drizzle over the cake – you could also pop a few nuts or dried fruit on top as a garnish.

This started out as a berry drizzle cake, then we adapted it for our gluten and wheat free customers. It's great to see folks sitting in the café eating homemade, gluten free cake that is moist and delicious rather than chewing their way through a heavy cardboard bought-in cake.

· This will keep for four days in an airtight container at room temperature.

· You can use fresh raspberries if you have them, but we use frozen because they are easier to mix through without smashing the berries up. Use any berries and citrus you like – experiment!

Gluten Free Raspberry and Orange Loaf

Serves 8

for the loaf:
250g caster sugar
250g butter
zest of 1 orange
1½ teaspoons vanilla extract
4 large eggs
250g gluten free plain flour
2 teaspoons gluten free
   baking powder
2 teaspoons xanthan gum
180g frozen raspberries

for the frosting:
180g cream cheese
290g icing sugar
70g butter, melted
zest of ½ orange

23 x 13cm loaf tin

Grease your tin and preheat your oven to 170°C (150°C fan). In a large bowl, cream the sugar, butter, orange zest and vanilla extract until fluffy and pale, either by hand or in a cake mixer with the balloon whisk attachment. This can take up to 15 minutes even in a mixer, so don't rush it. Add the eggs, one at a time, mixing for at least two to three minutes between each egg – don't add the eggs all at once. Sieve the flour, baking powder and xanthan gum into the bowl, then add the raspberries and mix through using your hand. Don't over-mix and don't mix the dry ingredients in with the cake mixer or you will end up with a heavy cake.

Scrape the batter into your prepared tin and bake near the bottom of the oven for 70 minutes until a skewer comes out clean. Leave the cake to cool in the tin on a rack. When the cake is completely cold, turn it out onto a serving plate. Put the cream cheese in a bowl with the icing sugar, melted butter and orange zest and mix (either by hand or with a mixer) until you have a glossy, smooth icing. Either spread it thickly on the top of the loaf, or use a piping bag with a large star nozzle to cover the top with rustic dots of icing.

We took a simple orange cake recipe and kept adapting it until we got this fabulous, moist, gluten and wheat free cake.

· You need a food processor for this one.

· You don't have to make this one gluten and wheat free – just use plain wheat flour and baking powder and leave out the xanthan gum.

· This will keep for four days in an airtight container at room temperature.

Italian Orange and Almond Cake

Serves 8

for the cake:
1 orange
230g dairy free margarine
  (we use Pure)
230g dark brown sugar
4 large eggs
230g gluten free plain flour
2½ teaspoons gluten free
  baking powder
1½ teaspoons xanthan gum
65g ground almonds

for the icing:
150g icing sugar
3–4 tablespoons lemon juice

20cm springform cake tin

Preheat your oven to 170°C (150°C fan) and grease your tin.

Zest your orange, then remove and discard the skin and pith. Cut the remaining flesh up into chunks. Put the zest and flesh into a food processor with the margarine and brown sugar. Blitz until you have a smooth paste, then add the eggs and blitz again till you have a weird-looking, separated liquid. Pour this out into a mixing bowl and sieve the flour, baking powder and xanthan gum over the top. Add the ground almonds. Using a wooden spoon, mix it thoroughly together, then pour the batter into your tin and bake for an hour or until a skewer comes out clean. Leave the cake to cool in the tin.

When the cake is completely cold, take it out of the tin and place on your serving plate. In a small bowl, mix your icing sugar and lemon juice to make a smooth, slightly runny icing. Drizzle the icing over the cake and, if you like, pop some flaked almonds and mixed peel on top.

A healthier flapjack that is super friendly for wheat free folks and vegans.

· This will keep for four days in an airtight container kept at room temperature.

· If you're not dairy free, you can use butter instead of margarine.

Flapjack

Serves 8

375g dairy free margarine
300g gluten and wheat free oats
300g gluten free plain flour
260g dark brown sugar
zest of 1 lemon
100g frozen blueberries
100g frozen raspberries
5 tablespoons demerara sugar

20cm springform cake tin

Preheat your oven to 170°C (150°C fan) and grease your tin.

Put the margarine in a mixing bowl with the oats, gluten free flour, dark brown sugar and lemon zest. Use your hands to mix the margarine evenly through the other ingredients until you have a thick, sticky dough with no lumps of margarine. Split the dough into three equal pieces. Push one piece into the bottom of the tin and smooth it out into an even layer. Scatter the frozen blueberries on top. Press another piece of dough in an even layer over the blueberries and smooth out. Scatter over the frozen raspberries. Press the last of the dough in a layer on top, smooth it out and sprinkle the demerara sugar on top. Bake for 50 to 60 minutes until it's golden brown and firm. Leave to cool in the tin, then slice into eight pieces and serve.

Banana and white chocolate is always a winning combination, but the addition of cherries adds a whole new bang to these muffins.

· We use large Texas muffin tins which are roughly double the size of standard ones. Use whichever you have handy.

· These are also good with pineapple or fresh berries instead of cherries.

· Muffins are best eaten the day you bake them, but they will keep for two days in an airtight container at room temperature. If you store them, try heating them up a little before you eat them – even a wee zap in the microwave softens them and brings the banana flavour back out.

Banana, Cherry and White Chocolate Muffins

Makes 6 large or 12 standard muffins

350g plain flour
1½ teaspoons baking powder
90g caster sugar
100g good quality
   white chocolate chips
110g tinned pitted cherries,
   drained
1 large banana, mashed
2 large eggs
250ml full fat milk
110g butter, melted

Texas or standard muffin tins

Preheat your oven to 170°C (150°C fan) and line your muffin tins with cases or greaseproof paper.

In a large mixing bowl, combine your plain flour, baking powder, sugar, white chocolate chips, cherries and mashed banana. In another bowl, whisk your eggs and milk together. Add the eggy milk mix to the first bowl and pour in your melted butter. Mix everything gently by hand – don't over-mix or you'll have heavy muffins, so be as gentle as possible.

Divide your batter between the muffin cases and bake for 30 minutes until they are golden brown and a skewer comes out clean. Remove from the pan straight away and leave to cool on a rack. A wee drizzle of melted white chocolate and a banana chip finishes these off beautifully.

Spicy chocolate muffins – you just can't beat them! These are awesome eaten still warm from the oven so you get runny chocolate chunks in each bite.

· We use large Texas muffin tins which are roughly double the size of standard ones. Use whichever you have.

· Muffins are best eaten the day you bake them, but they will keep for two days in an airtight container at room temperature. If you store them, try heating them up a little before you eat them – even a wee zap in the microwave softens them and brings the flavour back out.

Chocolate and Cardamom Muffins

Makes 6 large or 12 standard sized muffins

90g dark chocolate,
  roughly chopped
390g plain flour
260g caster sugar
3 teaspoons baking powder
¼ teaspoon bicarbonate of soda
60g cocoa powder
1 teaspoon ground cardamom
350ml full fat milk
110ml vegetable oil
1 large egg

Texas or standard muffin tins

Preheat your oven to 170°C or (150°C fan) and line your muffin pans with cases or greaseproof paper.

In a large mixing bowl, combine your dark chocolate chunks with the plain flour, caster sugar, baking powder, bicarbonate of soda, cocoa powder, and ground cardamom. In another bowl whisk together your milk, oil and egg. Add the milk mixture to the dry ingredients and gently fold with your hand until you have a smooth batter. Don't over-mix or you'll get heavy muffins; be as gentle as possible.

Divide your batter between the muffin cases and bake for 25 minutes until a skewer comes out clean. Remove from the tin straight away and leave the muffins to cool on a rack. We sit some more chocolate chips on top as soon as they come out of the oven or drizzle on a little extra melted chocolate, just for the naughtiness factor.

We came up with this recipe so we could offer veggie-friendly cheesecakes that didn't use gelatine or eggs. The result is incredibly light, chocolatey and rich with a real feel of decadence.

· If you are gluten or wheat free, use appropriate biscuits for the crumb.

· Don't add the chocolate ganache to the cream cheese mix while it's still hot – let it cool a little.

· Take care not to over-whip your cream or the cheesecake won't be as smooth. If it does go grainy and stiff, loosen the mix with a little un-whipped double cream.

· Try this out with other fruits; it's great using berries instead of the cherries.

· You can easily make this a white chocolate cheesecake: just use 320g best quality white chocolate and reduce the double cream to 90ml, and keep all the other ingredients the same. You will need to whip the cream a little stiffer to help the cheesecake set.

· This will keep in the fridge for up to five days.

Dark Chocolate and Cherry Cheesecake

Serves 8–10

for the base:
300g digestive biscuits
100g unsalted butter, melted

for the cheesecake:
300g dark chocolate,
  roughly chopped
120g double cream
375g cream cheese
60g sour cream
50g caster sugar
250ml double cream, whipped
4 tablespoons kirsch brandy
150g tinned pitted cherries,
  drained, plus a handful for
  the top
grated chocolate for the top

20cm springform cake tin

Grease your cake tin and line the base with greaseproof paper.

Grind your digestives to a fine crumb in a food processor (or put them in a plastic bag and bash them with a rolling pin). Put the biscuit crumbs into a mixing bowl and pour over the melted butter, then mix by hand until the butter is thoroughly mixed in. Tip this into the prepared tin and press it down to make a firm, even base. Pop in the fridge to set while you get the rest of the filling sorted.

Place your chocolate and double cream in a heavy-bottomed saucepan and melt them together over the lowest possible heat, stirring constantly. As soon as the chocolate is melted and the cream fully incorporated, take the pan off the heat and leave to cool. Put the cream cheese, sour cream and caster sugar into a mixing bowl and beat firmly until combined. In another bowl, whip your cream to soft peaks. Pour the melted chocolate over the cream cheese, then fold in the whipped cream and kirsch until everything is evenly mixed, smooth and glossy. Stir your cherries through, then pour the filling over the base and smooth out evenly in the tin. Decorate with some more cherries and a bit of grated chocolate. Leave the cheesecake to set in the fridge for at least four hours before you take it out of the tin.

Big Kev is a crazy, lanky, health-freaky, mountain-biking chef that worked for us and we love him to bits. He is an epic baker and a passionate chef. This is his baked blueberry cheesecake recipe, and it is a stunner!

· The oven temperature may seem really low, but it stops the cheesecake from cracking in the oven so go with it.

· When you take it out of the oven, it will still be very wobbly and you will think it's not cooked. It is fine! Let it cool at room temperature and then put it in the fridge overnight to let it set – don't cut into it before then. This keeps for up to four days in the fridge, covered in clingfilm so it doesn't take on flavours from other foods.

· To avoid any drips in the oven, put the cheesecake tin on a lipped baking tray while it's cooking in case the base oozes.

Kev's Baked Blueberry Cheesecake

Serves 8–10

---

for the base:

300g digestive biscuits

100g unsalted butter, melted

for the cheesecake:

1 vanilla pod, scraped

150g caster sugar

40g cornflour

640g cream cheese

3 large eggs

280ml double cream

200g fresh blueberries

20cm springform cake tin.

Preheat your oven to 120°C (100°C fan). Grease your cake tin and line the base with greaseproof paper.

Grind your digestives to a fine crumb in a food processor (or put them in a plastic bag and bash them with a rolling pin). Put the biscuit crumbs in a mixing bowl and pour over the melted butter. Mix with your hand until the butter is thoroughly mixed in. Tip into the prepared tin and press it down to make a firm, even base. Pop the tin in the fridge to set while you get the rest of the filling sorted.

Place the vanilla pulp, caster sugar, cornflour, cream cheese and eggs into a large mixing bowl and beat until fully combined – easiest done with an electric mixer on a medium speed. When the mix is smooth and has thickened, turn the mixer to a lower speed and slowly drizzle in the double cream. Beat until fully combined, then tip in the blueberries and gently stir them through. Pour the mix over the base and put the tin on a baking tray. Bake in the oven for 1½ hours.

Carefully take the cheesecake out of the oven – it will be very wobbly – and leave to cool. When it's cold, pop it in the fridge overnight to set. Serve with fresh blueberries or our blueberry compote.

Pavlova is a dessert that gets taken very seriously back home. It's often the conversation at barbecues and parties: 'How do you make yours? How do you get it marshmallowy in the middle and crispy on the top?' Pavlova rivalry is rife! But mine kept flopping so I kept working at it. This recipe is a combination of a couple of versions, one being my mum's. I also started heating the sugar before adding it to the eggs – it makes them much more stable so no more flopping pavlova! I think I have nailed it.

· Make sure the mixing bowl is totally clean and has no signs of grease, and the eggs whites have no flecks of yolk in them or they will never whip.

· Pour the sugar into the eggs slowly – don't just dump it in.

· If you want to make meringues rather than pavlova, just spoon or pipe individual rounds onto a lined baking tray. You'll probably get six to eight out of this recipe, depending how big you make them.

· The pavlova without the cream will keep for up to five days in an airtight container.

· Keep the yolks to make custard (page 292) or hollandaise sauce (page 277).

Pavlova

Serves 8

for the pavlova:
300g caster sugar
160g egg whites
   (from 4 or 5 eggs)
½ tablespoon white wine vinegar
½ tablespoon cornflour
½ tablespoon vanilla extract

for the topping:
300ml double cream
2 teaspoons icing sugar
1 vanilla pod, scraped
3 kiwi fruits, peeled and
   sliced into thin rounds
2 handfuls berries of your choice
a little grated chocolate

Preheat your oven to 190°C with no fan as this will blow the sugar around the oven. Sprinkle the caster sugar evenly on baking paper on a flat baking tray and put in the oven for exactly eight minutes.

Two minutes before your sugar is done, start beating the egg whites in a cake mixer or with an electric mixer on high. Make sure the mixing bowl is totally clean and has no signs of grease. Tip the warm sugar carefully into a jug and turn the oven down to 120°C (100°C fan).

Turn the mixer back on to a high speed and, while it is running, slowly pour in the sugar. When all the sugar is added, turn the mixer off and add the white wine vinegar, the cornflour and the vanilla. Turn the mixer back on to high and beat for six minutes, until the meringue has cooled a bit and is lovely and glossy.

Line a baking tray with a silicone mat or some non-stick baking paper. Spread the meringue in a circle about 20cm in diameter and 8cm high and bake for 1½ hours. Leave to cool on a wire rack. When the pavlova is cold, move it to a serving plate. Whip your cream, icing sugar and vanilla pulp together until only just whipped. Gently smooth it over the pavlova and decorate with slices of kiwi, berries and some grated chocolate.

Arguably the most famous New Zealand cookie, this is the perfect combination of a chocolatey, crunchy, moreish cookie.

· You can use the chocolate frosting on page 217 instead of chocolate ganache if you prefer something a bit sweeter. Or you could try a white chocolate ganache instead of the dark – it's really nice. Just replace the dark chocolate with good quality white chocolate chips.

· These will keep in an airtight container for up to seven days.

Afghan Cookies

Makes 9

250g butter, softened
110g caster sugar
225g plain flour
50g cocoa powder
50g cornflakes

for the ganache:
150g dark chocolate chips
100ml double cream
20g butter

Preheat the oven to 180°C (160°C fan). Grease and flour a large baking tray.

Beat the butter and sugar in a cake mixer on a high speed, stopping the mixer occasionally to scrape the mix off the sides of the bowl so it's evenly mixed. You will know it's ready when the mix is light in colour and fluffy. If you're making this by hand, soften the butter in the microwave, then put it in a mixing bowl with the sugar and cream with a whisk. Sieve the flour and cocoa together and add to the bowl along with the cornflakes. Gently mix until the dough leaves the sides of the bowl and makes a big lump of soft cookie dough. If you're not using a cake mixer, use your hands to fold in the dry ingredients.

Split the dough into nine equal balls and then shape into flattish cookies between your palms. Place on your prepared tray and bake for 15 minutes until the cookies begin to firm up. You will be able to twist them on the tray, but they will still be too soft to pick up. Leave them to cool and harden on the tray on a wire rack.

Place the chocolate, cream and butter in a heavy-bottomed pan and put over the lowest temperature possible. Keep stirring as everything melts together, then take off the heat as soon as you have a smooth ganache and keep stirring until it thickens. When the biscuits are completely cold, spoon a big dollop of the icing on top of each one. Make sure the ganache is cold and thick enough to spoon – otherwise it will slide straight off. Place a walnut half on top of each cookie, and leave to set.

Store in an airtight container or jar.

'Anzac' stands for Australia New Zealand Army Corp. These cookies are part of New Zealand and Australia's wartime history. Wives would use their rations to bake these delicious cookies, sending them by sea to their homesick hubbies. They do keep for ages in an airtight container. We have sexed them up with the addition of cranberries, pumpkin seeds and dried apricots.

· The dough may seem greasy and sticky but this is good! It mustn't be dry or crumbly or the cookies will fall apart.

· They spread quite a lot while baking so don't cram them on the baking tray.

· You can cook the dough as a slice like a flapjack if you prefer – just press it into a brownie tin. It's great with chocolate ganache on top.

· If you're going out on the hill, these are the perfect trail food.

· They will keep in an airtight container for up to ten days

Anzacs

Makes 8

120g butter
120g golden syrup
170g sugar
110g plain flour
80g desiccated coconut
100g rolled oats
100g dried cranberries
100g dried apricots,
  roughly chopped
25g pumpkin seeds
1½ teaspoons bicarbonate
  of soda

Preheat the oven to 170°C (150°C fan). Grease and lightly flour a couple of baking trays. Place your butter and golden syrup in a pan over a medium-low heat until the butter has melted into the hot syrup. Meanwhile, put the sugar, plain flour, coconut, oats, cranberries, apricots, pumpkin seeds and bicarbonate of soda into a large mixing bowl. Pour the hot butter/syrup mix into the bowl and stir until it is thoroughly mixed in and you have a big ball of dough.

Split the dough into eight evenly sized balls. Roll each one in your hands and pat down to make a cookie shape. Place, well-spaced, on your prepared trays. Bake for 15 minutes, then leave the cookies to harden on the tray and move them when they are cold and firm to an airtight container or jar.

It is compulsory to steal one while warm.

An old-fashioned Kiwi cookie that has been a kids' lunch box staple forever.

· If you don't have a cake mixer, use a hand-held electric mixer to cream the butter and sugar, then do the rest by hand.

· It's not compulsory but I love to add a wee drizzle of chocolate ganache to the top of these for extra cookie badness. Use the Afghan ganache recipe on page 210.

· You can keep the dough in the fridge for up to five days if you don't want to bake the whole batch in one go. To store, roll into a sausage shape and wrap in clingfilm. When you're ready to use the dough, unwrap and slice into even cookie rounds.

· The cookies keep for up to four days in an airtight container or jar.

Chocolate Chip Cookies

Makes 12

250g butter

170g sugar

180g condensed milk

½ teaspoon vanilla extract

480g plain flour

2 teaspoons baking powder

160g dark chocolate chips

160g white chocolate chips

Preheat oven to 180°C (160°C fan). Grease and lightly flour two baking trays. Put the butter, sugar, condensed milk and vanilla extract in a mixing bowl and beat either with a hand-held electric mixer or in a cake mixer on full speed until the mix is light, fluffy and pale in colour. Stop the mixer from time to time and scrape down the sides of the bowl to help dissolve the sugar evenly. It will take at least 10 minutes to be really well-creamed. Add the flour, baking powder and the chocolate chips to the bowl and mix until everything is fully combined and the dough comes together in one big lump in the bowl. Try not to over-mix or the chocolate chips will break up and stain the cookies brown when they bake.

Split the dough into 12 evenly sized pieces. Use the palm of your hand to roll and flatten each one into a cookie shape. Place onto the prepared baking trays and press down with the tines of a floured fork. If you are not cooking the whole batch, roll the remaining dough into a cylinder and wrap in clingfilm. Put it in the fridge until you need it and then just remove the clingfilm, slice into even rounds and cook as above – no need to mark them with a fork.

Bake for 20 minutes until lightly golden brown. Leave to harden on the tray for three to four minutes, then transfer to a rack to cool.

Buy chocolate biscuits? Why would you when you can make these simple and amazing melt-in-the-mouth chocolate biscuits?

· For a really cute and posh afternoon tea, make little tiny versions.

· These will keep for up to five days in an airtight container at room temperature.

Chocolate Melting Moments

Makes 6

---

for the biscuits:

290g butter, softened

90g icing sugar

½ teaspoon vanilla extract

300g plain flour

90g cornflour

60g cocoa powder

for the chocolate filling:

110g cream cheese

160g icing sugar

50g butter, melted

30g cocoa powder

Preheat your oven to 170°C (150°C fan). Grease and lightly flour two baking trays.

Put the butter, icing sugar and vanilla extract in a large mixing bowl and beat either with a hand-held electric mixer or in a cake mixer on full speed until the mix is light, fluffy and pale in colour. Stop the mixer from time to time and scrape down the sides of the bowl to help dissolve the sugar evenly. If you don't have a mixer, gently soften the butter in the microwave and use a whisk to cream it with the sugar. Add the flour, cornflour and cocoa to the bowl and beat until everything is well combined and you have a big lump of soft biscuit dough.

Split the dough into 12 even pieces and press each one between your hands to make a cookie shape. Place on the prepared baking trays and lightly fork the top of each biscuit. Bake for 15 minutes – you will be able to very gently pick them up off the tray when they're ready. Leave to cool on the tray. These biscuits are quite fragile, so be gentle with them once they're cooked.

Place all of the filling ingredients into a mixing bowl and beat together until you have a smooth, glossy frosting. Turn all the biscuits upside down and spoon the frosting onto the bases of six of them. Sandwich each one with an un-frosted biscuit. Leave to set on the tray for about 30 minutes so they don't slide apart.

Store in an airtight container or jar.

A perfect summer picnic biscuit with true class.

· These will keep in the airtight container for up to five days.

Passion Fruit Melting Moments

Makes 6

for the cookies:
250g salted butter, softened
95g icing sugar
½ teaspoon vanilla extract
300g plain flour
95g cornflour

for the passion fruit filling:
100g cream cheese
160g icing sugar
40g butter, melted
pulp of 1 passion fruit

Preheat your oven to 170°C (150°C fan). Grease and lightly flour two baking trays.

Put the butter, icing sugar and vanilla extract in a mixing bowl and beat either with a hand-held electric mixer or in a cake mixer on full speed until it is light, fluffy and pale in colour. Stop the mixer from time to time and scrape down the sides of the bowl to help dissolve the sugar evenly. If you don't have a mixer, gently soften the butter in the microwave and use a whisk to cream it with the sugar. Add the flour and cornflour and mix until you have a big lump of soft biscuit dough.

Split the dough into 12 evenly sized pieces and shape each one into a biscuit with your hands. Place on the prepared baking trays and lightly fork the top of each biscuit, then bake for 15 minutes. You will be able to very gently pick them up off the tray when they're ready – this is how we test them. Leave the biscuits to cool on the tray; they are quite fragile, so be gentle once baked.

Place the cream cheese, icing sugar, melted butter and passion fruit pulp into a mixing bowl and beat together until you have a smooth, glossy frosting. Turn all the biscuits upside down and spoon filling onto six of them, then sandwich with the un-frosted biscuits. Dust the tops with a little more icing sugar and leave to set on the tray for 30 minutes so they don't slide apart. Store in an airtight container or jar.

This was the first thing I ever baked at the café. When we first took over, we inherited an old gas oven that was pretty temperamental and awful for baking in. My badass brownie was perfected in that oven (with a lot of fails and swear words) and is now one of our best sellers. I love it because all you need is a saucepan and a wooden spoon to make it.

· This will keep in an airtight container for up to five days. It won't last that long though!

· I have a standard joke with the chefs about checking if the brownies are cooked: if it's firm and soft like boobs it's ready; if it's wobbly and soft like my belly it's not ready.

Kj's Badass Chocolate Brownies

Makes 12 generous slices

340g dark chocolate,
  roughly chopped
250g butter
675g caster sugar
4 large eggs
1 teaspoon vanilla extract
450g plain flour

25 x 20cm brownie tin

Preheat the oven to 170°C (150°C fan). Grease and line your tin with greaseproof paper.

Put the chocolate and butter in a heavy-bottomed saucepan large enough to take all the ingredients. Place on a low heat until they're fully melted with no lumps, stirring as they melt. Remove from the heat and leave to cool till you can hold your finger in the mix. Add the sugar, eggs and vanilla extract and beat really well with a wooden spoon until smooth and shiny. Sieve the flour and fold it in to get a very thick batter. Scrape it into the lined tin and smooth out with a spatula. Bake for 25 minutes until the brownie is firm around the edges and still a little soft in the middle. Leave to cool in the tin at room temperature before cutting – we leave ours overnight to make sure we get a nice, clean-cut slice.

This is my favourite home-bake at the café. You will often see me in the late afternoon, sneaking out the front with a stolen piece or I'll sometimes save it for the drive home. It's the bomb of brownies. It's also a one-pot-wonder: all you need is a pot and a wooden spoon to make it!

- We use frozen raspberries as they don't break up while you're mixing and you get lush big lumps of them in the blondie. If you're using fresh ones, be careful not to over-mix them.

- Use the best quality white chocolate you can find.

- Try walnuts or pecans instead of the macadamia nuts.

- This is a brownie so it still wants to be a little wobbly when it comes out of the oven – you can't check it with a skewer

- These keep for four days in an airtight container at room temperature.

- **Warning:** Highly Addictive!

Raspberry, White Chocolate and Macadamia Blondie

Makes 10 generous slices

300g white chocolate chips
160g butter, diced
240g caster sugar
3 large eggs
1 teaspoon vanilla extract
165g plain flour
125g self-raising flour
100g white chocolate,
   roughly chopped
150g frozen raspberries
80g macadamia nuts,
   roughly chopped

25 x 20cm brownie tin

Preheat the oven to 170°C (150°C fan). Grease and line the tin with the greaseproof paper.

Put the white chocolate chips and the butter in a heavy-bottomed saucepan large enough to take all the ingredients. Melt, stirring, on a low heat until everything is fully melted with no lumps. Remove from the heat and leave to cool till you can hold your finger in the mix. Add the sugar, eggs and vanilla extract and beat really well with a wooden spoon until you have a smooth, shiny mix. Add the plain and self-raising flours, roughly chopped white chocolate, raspberries and macadamias. Fold gently until you have a thick brownie batter.

Scrape it into the lined tin and smooth out with a spatula, then bake for 30 minutes, until golden brown, firm at the edges but still a little wobbly in the middle. It needs to sit for a good few hours to firm up before you cut it, ideally overnight.

We churn out roughly 86 slices a week of this in the busy summer months. It does take time and patience – it is not a quick, whip-together recipe – but it is so worth the effort.

· Make sure you take the label off the condensed milk tin before you boil it or the glue will knacker your saucepan!

· Be careful not to let the tin boil dry as it will explode. No one wants that in their kitchen...

· When you open the hot tin of condensed milk, stab a hole with the tin opener first to release the pressure and avoid burns.

· This will keep in the fridge for up to ten days.

Millionaires' Shortbread

Makes 12 generous slices

for the caramel:

1 x 397g tin of condensed milk

250g salted butter

140g caster sugar

for the base:

330g butter, softened

190g dark brown sugar

350g plain flour

120g cornflour

for the chocolate topping:

400g good quality
  dark chocolate chips

300g double cream

100g butter

30 x 23cm brownie tin

Place the unopened tin of condensed milk, minus its label, in a small deep saucepan. Cover it completely with hot water and boil for four hours, topping up with water so the tin is covered all the time.

Preheat the oven to 170°C (150°C fan). Grease and line your tin with greaseproof paper.

To make the base: cream the butter and sugar until paler in colour and light and fluffy. Scrape down the sides of the bowl occasionally to help with even mixing. Add the flour and cornflour and mix through until you have one lump of dough. Scrape the dough into your tray and squash it down with your hands to get a roughly even layer. Dip a pallet knife in hot water and run it over the top to smooth out the base (a bit of hot water helps move the dough around, but don't overdo it). Bake for 20 minutes, until the base is lightly browned, puffy and biscuity. Set aside to cool.

Now start on the caramel. Once your tin of condensed milk has boiled for four hours, drain off the water. Leave the tin to cool for about ten minutes so it doesn't burst when you pierce it with a tin opener, then stab a hole with the opener to release any pressure. Put the butter and sugar in a heavy-bottomed saucepan. Fully open the tin and scrape the hot contents into the pan. Place on a high heat and whisk vigorously until the butter melts and the sugar combines with the condensed milk. Keep whisking constantly as the caramel comes to the boil: it will look smooth, thick and volcanic. Be really careful doing this – it can splatter. We sometimes use a stick blender instead of a whisk as it moves the caramel around fast, gets rid of any lumps and gives you a really silky finish. Pour the caramel over your cooled base and leave to set.

To make the chocolate topping, melt the chocolate, cream and butter in a heavy-bottomed saucepan over the lowest heat possible. Stir constantly as it melts and take the pan off the heat as soon as everything is smooth and fully combined. Make sure your tin is on a flat surface and pour the topping over the cold caramel. Leave to set overnight, then cut into 12 slices.

I started making Ginger Crunch at the café for purely sentimental reasons. On a visit home, I was having a barbecue with my good school friend Karen and her parents. After a few glasses of Sauv Blanc, stories of our teenage years started to flow and Karen's dad, Paddy, would jump in and say, 'Ginger Crunch anyone?' every time he felt uncomfortable – which was a lot. It was hilarious. As soon as I returned to the café it went on the cake counter and it always makes me smile.

· The base will puff up really high when you bake it, then collapse and look a bit cracked and ugly. Don't worry, this always happens! While it's still warm, push the sides down to make an even layer and leave it to cool.

· This keeps for five days in an airtight container at room temperature. It goes stale in the fridge.

Ginger Crunch

Makes 12 generous slices

for the base:

270g butter, softened

225g caster sugar

300g plain flour

2 teaspoons ground ginger

1 teaspoon baking powder

for the icing:

200g golden syrup

100g butter

375g icing sugar

6 teaspoons ground ginger

a handful of unsalted pistachios,
  roughly chopped (optional)

25 x 20cm brownie tin

Preheat your oven to 180°C (160°C fan). Grease and line your tin with greaseproof paper.

Put the butter and sugar in a mixing bowl and cream with an electric mixer or a whisk until pale, light and fluffy. Stop and scrape down the sides of the bowl occasionally to help with even mixing. Add the flour, ginger and baking powder and mix through to make a wet shortbread dough. Scrape the dough into your tray, smooth out with a spatula and bake for 15 to 20 minutes, until it is puffy and lightly golden brown. Leave to cool and firm up, pressing down the sides to make an even base while it's still warm.

Once the base is cool, place your golden syrup and butter in a heavy-bottomed saucepan, then add the icing sugar and ginger. Melt on the lowest heat possible, stirring, until everything is combined and you have a smooth, runny icing. Take it off the heat and whisk until the icing starts to thicken. Pour it evenly over the base – make sure your tin is sitting on a flat surface. Sprinkle a few pistachio nuts on top if you want, then leave to set. When the icing is firm enough to cut, peel away the greaseproof paper and slice into 12 pieces.

My mum used to make the best coconut rough ever! However, I've adapted her recipe and it just might give her a run for her money... I've used a ganache topping instead of her chocolate icing and it is outrageous with the coconut.

· The rough is a bit like a cookie dough to cook – it still wants to be a little soft when you take it out of the oven as it will firm up when it cools.

· If you're not into the richness of the chocolate ganache topping, use a double quantity of the chocolate filling on page 217.

· The base must be absolutely cold before you pour on the warm ganache.

· This keeps for five days in an airtight container at room temperature. It goes stale in the fridge.

· At the café, we sometimes use other nuts instead of coconut to mix it up: pistachios work really well, so do pecans. Use roughly 60g roughly chopped nuts to replace the desiccated coconut.

Coconut Rough

Makes 12 generous slices

for the base:

170g butter, softened

175g dark brown sugar

1 teaspoon vanilla extract

1 large egg

35g self-raising flour

150g plain flour

3 tablespoons cocoa powder

80g desiccated coconut

for the topping:

280g dark chocolate,
   roughly chopped

180g double cream

20g desiccated coconut

25 x 20cm brownie tin

Preheat your oven to 180°C (160°C fan). Grease and line your tin with greaseproof paper

Cream the butter, sugar and vanilla extract until light, fluffy and pale brown in colour. Scrape down the sides of the bowl often to help with even mixing. You can use an electric mixer or a whisk for this – just make sure your butter is well softened. Beat in the egg, again scraping the sides of the bowl to ensure it is evenly mixed through. Add the self-raising and plain flours, cocoa powder and coconut and mix through until you have a lump of soft dough. Scrape the dough into your tin, smooth it out with a spatula and bake for 14 minutes. Leave to cool.

When the base is completely cold, make the topping: place your dark chocolate and double cream into a heavy-bottomed saucepan and melt together on the lowest possible heat. Keep stirring until it's almost completely melted, then take off the heat and stir until smooth and glossy. Pour the ganache evenly over the base and sprinkle the coconut over the top. Leave to set, then peel away the greaseproof paper and cut into 12 slices.

Our front of house team go crazy when we make this slice and it almost needs to be policed when they're cutting it. I'm pretty sure only about half of what we bake gets to the cake counter due to front of house gluttony...

· If you want to make this gluten or wheat free, use gluten or wheat free biscuits for the base.

· This keeps for five days in an airtight container at room temperature. It goes stale in the fridge.

· The slice will seem quite soft and gooey when it comes out of the oven but don't worry – the condensed milk caramel sets as it cools.

Baked Caramel Nut Slice

Makes 10 generous slices

200g digestive biscuits
100g unsalted butter, melted
100g dark chocolate chips
50g desiccated coconut
50g flaked almonds
50g pistachios
50g pecans
50g dried cranberries
30g ground almonds
400g condensed milk

25 x 20cm brownie tin

Preheat your oven to 180°C (160°C fan). Grease and line your brownie tin.

Blitz the digestives in a food processor until they are finely ground, then evenly sprinkle the crumbs into the lined tin. Gently pour the melted butter all over the crumbs and let it soak in. Put the chocolate chips, coconut, flaked almonds, pistachios, pecans, cranberries and ground almonds in a large bowl and mix together, then press over the biscuit base in an even layer. Slowly drizzle the condensed milk all over the top and leave to soak in for five minutes. Bake for about 25 minutes, until golden brown.

Leave the slice to cool and firm up in the tin, then take it out and peel off the paper. Some paper often sticks to the sides so just trim the edges with a knife, then cut it up into ten pieces.

This super-easy fridge slice is a great one for if you are limited on time, but want to make something sexy. You can whip this up and have it in the fridge setting within 15 minutes.

· This keeps for seven days in the fridge.

· Try using freeze-dried berries instead of the cranberries for a super yummy summer slice.

· Keep any leftover condensed milk to make our Old School Salad Dressing recipe on page 83.

Custard, White Chocolate and Cranberry Fridge Slice

Makes 10 generous slices

---

for the base:
125g butter
200g condensed milk
2 teaspoons custard powder
220g custard cream biscuits,
  plus some for the top
25g dried cranberries,
  plus some for the top
80g good quality
  white chocolate chips

for the topping:
300g good quality
  white chocolate chips
150ml double cream
white chocolate shavings
  for the top

25 x 20cm brownie tin

Grease and line the tin with greaseproof paper.

In a saucepan, melt the butter, condensed milk and custard powder on a low heat. Use a whisk to make sure all the custard powder dissolves. Put the biscuits in a large mixing bowl and smash with the end of a rolling pin until you have small pieces. Add the cranberries and white chocolate chips, then pour over the hot condensed milk and stir thoroughly to combine. Scrape the mix out into your lined tin and press it down to make a well-packed base.

Now make the topping. In a heavy-bottomed saucepan, melt the white chocolate with the double cream over the lowest possible heat. Pour this over the biscuit base and decorate with some more whole custard creams, cranberries and white chocolate shavings. Put in the fridge and leave for a couple of hours or until the topping is firm enough to cut. Remove the paper and cut into 12 slices. Keep in the fridge.

Super-quick, simple, easy and totally naughty. Put your own take on this recipe by using your favourite chocolates or chocolate bars: we have used everything from Aero, Snickers and Ferrero Rocher to Bounty and Turkish Delight.

· If you want to go chocolate-mental, use bourbon creams in the base.

· Keep this slice in the fridge; it will keep for seven days.

· Keep any leftover condensed milk to make our Old School NZ Salad Dressing on page 83.

Dark Chocolate Fridge Slice

Makes 10 generous slices

for the base:
125g butter
200g condensed milk
220g digestive or
   rich tea biscuits
3 chocolate bars of your choice,
   roughly chopped (about 100g)
50g dark chocolate chips

for the ganache topping:
225g dark chocolate chips
250ml double cream

25 x 20cm brownie tin

Grease and line the tin with greaseproof paper.

In a saucepan, melt the butter and condensed milk over a low heat. Put the biscuits in a large bowl and smash them with the end of a rolling pin until you have small pieces. Add two-thirds of the chopped chocolate bars and the chocolate chips. Pour the hot condensed milk over the biscuit mix and stir it through thoroughly. Scrape out into your lined tin and push it down to make an even, well-packed base.

For the topping, put the dark chocolate and double cream in a heavy-bottomed saucepan and melt, stirring, over the lowest possible heat. Once you have a smooth and glossy ganache, pour it evenly over the biscuit base. Sprinkle the remaining chopped chocolate bar on top and pop in the fridge until the ganache topping has set – about three hours. Remove the paper and cut into ten slices.

This is my favourite Nana recipe – it's been part of my life for as long as I can remember. My husband nicknamed it 'Nana's heroin slice' because of its addictiveness. On arriving home every year there would be tins of the stuff to go with endless cups of tea we had with her. She made us a double batch once for a climbing trip in the Southern Alps – it fuelled our whole trip and I'm amazed we weren't diabetic by the time we returned.

· Make this gluten or wheat free by using appropriate biscuits.

· This keeps for seven days in the fridge.

Nana's Coffee and Walnut Slice

Makes 16 generous slices

for the base:
175g butter
250g condensed milk
1½ tablespoons instant coffee granules
250g rich tea biscuits
100g walnut halves, roughly chopped, plus a handful for the top
90g desiccated coconut, plus a handful for the top

for the topping:
1 tablespoon instant coffee granules
1 tablespoon boiling water
170g cream cheese
60g butter, melted
370g icing sugar

30 x 23cm brownie tin

Grease and line the tin with greaseproof paper.

Melt the butter, condensed milk and coffee granules together in a saucepan over a low heat, using a whisk to make sure all the coffee granules dissolve. Put the biscuits in a large mixing bowl and smash with the end of a rolling pin until you have small pieces – they want to be small chunks, not fine crumbs. Add your walnuts and desiccated coconut, then pour over the hot condensed milk and stir thoroughly. Scrape out into your lined tin and press down to make a well-packed base. Leave aside while you make your topping.

Put the instant coffee in a small bowl, then add the boiling water and stir till the granules have dissolved. Put your cream cheese, melted butter and icing sugar in a mixing bowl and add the coffee. Beat until everything is combined to make a smooth, glossy and fluffy icing. Spoon this over the biscuit base and smooth out with a spatula, then sprinkle with walnut pieces and some desiccated coconut as a garnish. Leave to set in the fridge for a couple of hours before cutting into 16 slices.

Big slabs of set chocolate with fluffy marshmallows, crunchy nuts and chewy fruits: the perfect snack to fuel a day on the hill.

· This will keep in the fridge for up to 14 days in the greaseproof roll.

· You can use a small loaf or brownie tin lined with greaseproof paper to shape the rocky road if you don't fancy trying the rolling method below.

Rocky Road

Makes 10 slices

170g good quality white
  or dark chocolate
45g butter
20g pistachios
20g flaked almonds
20g glacé cherries
20g dried cranberries
20g sultanas
20g dried apricots, chopped
100g large marshmallows

Melt the chocolate and butter together over a low heat in a heavy-bottomed saucepan. Take off the heat and stir in the pistachios, almonds, cherries, cranberries, sultanas, apricots and marshmallows. Leave to cool and firm up for about 10 to 15 minutes.

Take a piece of greaseproof paper about 30cm long and lay it on the workbench, longest side closest to you. Scrape the cooled chocolate mix in a sausage shape about 20cm long in the middle of the paper. Take the bottom of the greaseproof paper and fold it over the mix, smoothing it with your hands to make a log. Carefully roll your log away from you so it is snugly wrapped up in the paper, then twist the ends to keep it tight. Pop the log in the fridge to set for about four hours and cut into 2cm thick slabs to serve.

After a sea kayaking and climbing trip to Cornwall in 2013, I became a total scone snob and am now totally addicted to clotted cream. Scones and cream teas became part of our five-a-day on that holiday. I came home determined to make our scones better and get clotted cream on the menu.

- The more the butter is mixed into the flour, the better; you cannot overdo this part of mixing the scones. Make sure you have a proper breadcrumb consistency with no lumps of butter.

- Cut the dough with a quick up-and-down motion, being careful not to drag the knife. This helps them rise evenly and prevents lopsided scones!

- They say you should never have to cut a good scone; it should split easily in your hands.

- These are best eaten on the day you bake them, so I don't recommend storing them.

Sweet Scones

Makes 6

300g self-raising flour
65g caster sugar
75g butter, cut into small cubes
110ml full fat milk
1 large egg

Preheat your oven to 180°C (160°C fan). Grease and flour a large baking tray.

Put the flour and sugar in a large mixing bowl and rub the butter in with your fingertips until you get a fine breadcrumb consistency. If you have a cake mixer, mix on a low speed with the paddle beater. Pour the milk into a small bowl and whisk in the egg. Pour this into the flour/sugar/butter crumbs and mix in to get a soft ball of dough – go easy at this stage as over-mixing will result in hard, heavy scones, so be as light and gentle as you can.

Place the dough on a floured worktop and gently shape into a smooth ball. Lightly flour the top, then roll it out to 4cm thick. With a sharp knife, cut six scones from the dough and put them on the prepared baking tray. Bake for 25 minutes till golden brown – to see if they are ready, lightly lift off the top of a scone and check the inside is cooked and not at all doughy. Serve with clotted cream or butter and your favourite jam!

VARIATIONS
There's no limit to what you can add to your scone dough to vary the flavour. Add the extra ingredients once you have made your dough – scatter them on top and gently knead through. If you are adding wet ingredients like fresh berries you will need to add an extra dusting of self-raising flour or the dough will be too sticky to work with. Here are some of our favourite combinations:

· ½ apple, roughly chopped & ¾ teaspoon ground cinnamon
· 50g fresh berries & 50g chocolate chips
· 75g sultanas or dried cranberries.

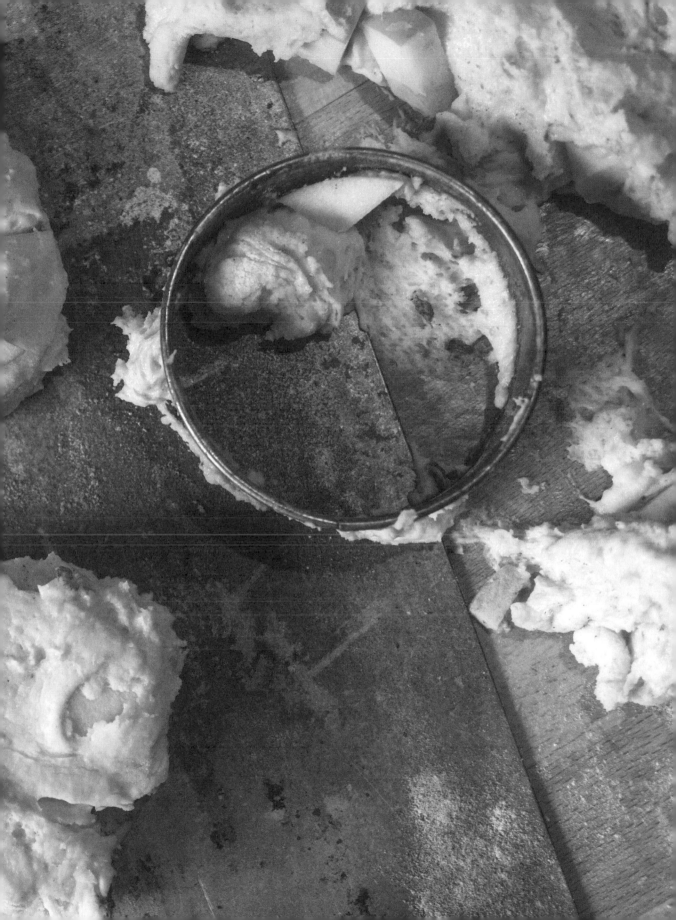

'You cannae beat a good scone!' is what our manager Claire says, much to our amusement! This recipe is top notch; these savoury scones would make my nana grin from ear to ear and that's saying something – she was a total savoury scone snob.

· The more the butter is mixed into the flour, the better; you cannot over do this part of mixing the scones. Make sure you have a proper breadcrumb consistency with no lumps of butter.

· Cut the dough with a quick up-and-down motion, being careful not to drag the knife. This helps them rise evenly and prevents lopsided scones!

· They say you should never have to cut a good scone; it should easily split apart in your hands. These are best eaten on the day you bake them, so I wouldn't recommend storing them.

Red Onion, Cheddar and Chive Savoury Scones

Makes 9

450g self-raising flour
1 teaspoon fine sea salt
1 teaspoon cracked black pepper
125g butter, cut into small cubes
190g mature Cheddar, grated
1 small red onion,
  quartered and finely sliced
10g chives, finely chopped
60g spinach, roughly chopped
210ml full fat milk
1 large egg

Preheat your oven to 180°C (160°C fan). Grease and flour a large baking tray.

Put the flour, salt and pepper in a large mixing bowl and rub the butter in with your fingertips until you get a fine breadcrumb consistency. If you have a cake mixer, mix on a low speed with the paddle beater. Add 100g of the grated cheese, red onion, chives and spinach and mix through by hand. Pour the milk into a small bowl and whisk in the egg. Pour this into the bowl of dry ingredients and mix in to get a soft ball of dough – go easy at this stage as over-mixing will result in hard, heavy scones, so be as light and gentle as you can and stop as soon as the liquid is incorporated.

Place the dough on a well-floured tabletop and gently knead to a smooth ball. Lightly flour the top and roll out to 4cm thick. With a sharp knife, cut nine scones from the dough and put on the prepared baking tray. Sprinkle each one with the remaining grated cheese and bake for 25 minutes till golden brown and cooked through. To see if the scones are ready, gently lift the lid of one and check that it isn't at all doughy in the middle.

Serve warm with butter and your favourite relish!

Aggie, our lovely wee Polish chef, was with us for six years – a true friend, family member and inspiration. I have never met anyone so stubborn, determined and talented. Aggie was my sous chef, and really helped me to get the kitchen where it is now. She trained in Ireland and that's where she picked up this delicious soda bread recipe.

· You can use natural yogurt instead of buttermilk.

· The loaf will keep for four days in an airtight container or well wrapped.

· It also freezes well. Wrap it in clingfilm, but unwrap before you defrost so it doesn't go soggy.

Aggie's Soda Bread

Makes 1 small loaf

110g self-raising flour
110g wholemeal flour
50g oats, plus some for the top
1 teaspoon bicarbonate of soda
1 teaspoon sea salt
¼ teaspoon cracked black pepper
50g unsalted butter, softened
1 large egg
225ml buttermilk

23 x 13cm loaf tin

Preheat your oven to 180°C (160°C fan). Grease and lightly flour the loaf tin.

Sieve the self-raising flour into a large bowl, then add the wholemeal flour, oats, bicarb, salt and black pepper. Rub the butter into the dry ingredients with your fingertips until it's fully dispersed and you have a crumbly consistency. In a small bowl, whisk the eggs and buttermilk together until smooth, then pour it into the crumbly flour mix. Stir it through until you have a sticky dough. Scrape the dough into the prepared tin and smooth down the top, then sprinkle a handful of oats over the top and bake for 40 minutes or until a skewer comes out clean. Tip the loaf straight out onto a rack to cool so it doesn't sweat in the tin.

Bread

Making bread is easy and will give you the best bread you have ever tasted. There are a few things you can do to make it even easier though:

When making your pre-fermented bread doughs, always add the water to the mixing bowl before the flour. It lubricates the bowl and helps disperse the flour evenly, so your final dough will be less lumpy.

We use active dried yeast in all our bread recipes. We don't hydrate or activate it in water – we just put it in with our flour.

Different flours have different properties, so you will find a wholemeal or rye flour proves much quicker than a white flour. Keep this in mind when you bake.

If it's your first time making bread, give yourself a break and bake it in a loaf tin. This will help your confidence grow, as you won't need to worry about shaping the dough and it will still taste great. If you're a keen baker, it's worth buying yourself a proving basket. It takes all the hassle out of shaping your loaves and trying to keep them in a round shape on a baking cloth.

Your dough will be affected by the temperature of your kitchen. If the room is really cold, the dough will prove slower and if the room is really warm, the dough may prove really fast. If it's not doing much or is slow to rise, you may need to move it to a warmer part of the room. If it's super warm and your dough is rising quickly, you will need to reduce your proving times. To check if the dough is proved and ready to go in the oven, poke your finger gently into the top of the loaf and the dough will spring back to the shape it was quite quickly. If it still feels very firm, it needs longer proving. If your finger goes straight into it, it is over-proved.

We knead and shape all our doughs on a large wooden butcher's board. If our kitchen is cold, the metal worktops will be too and you don't want to shock the bread by scraping it out onto a cold worktop. Plastic or Formica worktops tend to be fine – it's just cold metal you want to avoid.

To get a better crust on your bread that stays crisp longer, you need steam in your oven. Buy yourself a spray bottle from the hardware shop, fill it with water, and spray into the oven before you put your loaf in and a few times during baking. Never spray directly onto your bread, direct it towards the roof or sides of the oven.

This is the sexiest bread on the planet. I learnt to make it in Tuscany on a wee foodie cookery holiday a few years ago. Serve it warm with really good olive oil and you're cooking with gas!

· This recipe uses a poolish, or prefermented sponge, which is made the night before and then incorporated into your dough. It needs to stand for at least 12 to 16 hours. Using a poolish strengthens the structure of your dough, gives it a much better flavour and helps the bread last longer.

· The actual preparation of the dough takes three hours, but the finished bread is so worth the wait!

· You can use white spelt flour instead of wheat flour if you prefer – it works just the same.

Ciabatta

Makes 1 large loaf or 2 small ones

for the poolish
or preferment sponge:
240ml warm water
240g plain flour
2g active dried yeast

for the dough:
240ml warm water
400g plain flour
18g active dried yeast
16g salt
1½ tablespoons olive oil

To make the poolish, place the warm water in a mixing bowl, then add the flour and yeast. Mix vigorously with your hand for 5 to 10 minutes, until you have a dough that is becoming smooth and almost shiny. Tip into a clean and lightly oiled bowl or tub and cover with a tea towel. Leave to stand for 12 to 16 hours at room temperature. When the poolish is ready, it will have risen and be bubbly-looking, and it will smell a little fermented and beery.

The next morning, start on the dough. Put the warm water in a large mixing bowl. Add your bubbly poolish and the flour, yeast, salt and olive oil. Mix in with your hand until you have smooth bread dough. It will seem a bit loose and runny at this point, but don't worry! Vigorously knead for another five minutes, until the dough feels elastic and smooth. Tip the dough into a large, clean, well-oiled mixing bowl and leave to stand for an hour, covered with a tea towel.

After the hour is up, wet your hands with water and slide them underneath the dough on the far side of the bowl. Stretch the dough up and towards you. Do the same with the dough nearest you, stretching it up and towards the far side of the bowl. This is called 'putting a fold' into the dough. Cover the bowl again and leave for another hour, then repeat the folding process. Again cover the bowl and leave it for one more hour. By now the dough will feel firmer and easier to handle, but it may still seem quite wet compared to a normal bread dough.

Preheat your oven to 200°C (180°C fan) and grease your baking tray. When the dough has had its final hour of proving, gently tip it out onto a well-floured worktop. You can either cut it into two loaves or leave it as one. Either way, gently shape the dough with your hands into a long rectangular shape. Sprinkle a little flour on top and lift onto the prepared baking tray. Just before you put your bread in the oven, open the oven door and spray about five squirts of water inside to create some steam. Put in your bread and give the oven another spray after five minutes. Be careful not to spray directly onto the bread, but onto the walls of the oven. After five more minutes, spray again, then bake for another 10 to 15 minutes until the bread is golden brown. The total baking time is 20 to 25 minutes. Cool on a wire rack.

TIMELINE

· Make poolish, leave for 12 to 16 hours
· Make dough, prove for an hour
· Make first fold, prove for an hour
· Make second fold, prove for an hour
· Shape the loaf and spray water in oven
· Bake loaf for five minutes
· Spray water in oven, bake for another five minutes
· Spray water in oven, bake for a further 10 to 15 minutes

The first time I made focaccia was in a proper outdoor pizza oven in Italy on an epic travel and cooking trip. I have been trying to recreate that crust and flavour ever since, and this recipe is as close as it gets. For the best sandwiches ever, slap some crispy bacon, mayo, lettuce and avocado in between a couple of slices while it's still warm.

Focaccia Bread

Serves 4–6

320ml warm water

450g plain strong flour

16g dried active yeast

7g salt

1 teaspoon mixed dried herbs

2 tablespoons olive oil,
  plus more for the top

½ red onion, cut into 3cm
  pieces (optional)

10 cherry tomatoes

4 sprigs rosemary, cut into
  3cm pieces

sea salt

25 x 20cm brownie tin

Place your warm water into a large mixing bowl, then add your flour, yeast, salt, dried herbs and olive oil. Mix with your hand for about ten minutes until you have a smooth wet dough. Place the dough in a clean, well-oiled bowl and cover with a damp clean tea towel for 30 minutes.

After 30 minutes, wet your hands with water and slide them underneath the dough on the far side of the bowl. Stretch the dough up and towards you. Do the same with the dough nearest you, stretching it up and towards the far side of the bowl. This is called 'putting a fold' into the dough. Cover the bowl and leave at room temperature for an hour.

Lightly grease your brownie tin. Tip the dough out into the tin and push it down into an even layer. Cover with the damp tea towel and leave to prove for 20 minutes, then poke the red onion pieces (if you're using them), the whole cherry tomatoes and the rosemary sprigs into the loaf. Cover again and leave the dough to rest for 20 minutes. Preheat your oven to 200°C (180°C fan).

Just before you put your bread in the oven, open the oven door and spray about five squirts of water inside to create some steam. Put in your bread and give the oven another spray after five minutes – be careful not to spray directly onto the bread, but onto the walls of the oven. After five more minutes, spray again, then bake for another 10 to 15 minutes until the bread is golden brown. The total baking time is 20 to 25 minutes.

Once the bread is ready, brush more olive oil onto the hot bread and sprinkle with sea salt.

TIMELINE

· Make dough, prove for 30 minutes
· Make first fold, prove for an hour
· Shape in tin, prove for 20 minutes
· Poke in onion, tomatoes and rosemary, prove for 20 minutes
· Spray water in oven, bake for five minutes
· Spray water in oven, bake for another five minutes
· Spray water in oven, bake for a further 10 to 15 minutes
· Brush with oil and sprinkle with salt

This is the kind of bread that once you start eating, you can't stop... You have been warned! You can add anything to this bread, not just cranberries and fennel seeds. Apricot and poppy seeds are really good, or we sometimes crumble in some cooked black pudding with chopped sage.

Cranberry and Fennel French Loaves

Makes 1 loaf

230ml warm water
330g plain strong flour
12g dried active yeast
2 teaspoons salt
1 teaspoon sugar
75g dried cranberries
1 tablespoon fennel seeds

Place your water into a large mixing bowl and add your flour, yeast, salt, sugar, dried cranberries and fennel seeds. Mix with your hand for about 10 minutes until you have smooth dough. Place into a clean, well-oiled bowl and cover with a damp clean tea towel, then leave to rest at room temperature.

After 30 minutes, wet your hands with water and slide them underneath the dough on the far side of the bowl. Stretch the dough up and towards you. Do the same with the dough nearest you, stretching it up and towards the far side of the bowl. This is called 'putting a fold' into the dough. Cover again and leave for another 30 minutes. Repeat the folding process, cover, and leave for 20 minutes.

Tip the dough out onto a well-floured worktop and shape it into a smooth, round loaf. Place it onto a greased and floured baking tray or into a cloth-lined proving basket and cover with the damp tea towel. Leave to prove for one hour.

Preheat your oven to 200°C (180°C fan). Just before you put your bread in the oven, open the oven door and spray about five squirts of water inside to create some steam. Put in your bread and give the oven another spray after five minutes – be careful not to spray directly onto the bread, but onto the walls of the oven.

After five more minutes, spray again, then bake for another 10 to 15 minutes until the bread is golden brown. The total baking time is 20 to 25 minutes. Leave to cool on a wire rack.

TIMELINE

· Make dough, prove for 30 minutes
· Make first fold, prove for 30 minutes
· Make second fold, rest for 20 minutes
· Shape loaf, prove for one hour
· Spray water in oven, bake for five minutes
· Spray water in oven, bake for another five minutes
· Spray water in oven, bake for a further 10 to 15 minutes

To experience a slice of heaven, serve this warm or toasted with pastrami, American mustard, mayo and pickles!

Caraway and Rye Bread

Makes 1 large loaf or 2 small ones

370ml warm water
320g plain strong flour
210g rye flour
12g yeast
2 teaspoons salt
1 teaspoon caraway seeds

Place your water into a large mixing bowl and add your wheat and rye flours, yeast, salt and caraway seeds. Mix and knead with your hands for 15 minutes until you have smooth but sticky dough. Place into a clean, well-oiled bowl and cover with a damp clean tea towel for one hour. Shape the dough into a smooth round ball or rectangle and put it onto a greased and floured baking tray. Cover with a damp tea towel and leave to prove for 30 minutes.

Preheat your oven to 200°C (180°C fan). Using a sharp knife, make 4 long scores on the top of the dough and leave for about 10 minutes. Just before you put your bread in the oven, open the oven door and spray about five squirts of water inside to create some steam. Put in your bread and give the oven another spray after five minutes – be careful not to spray directly onto the bread, but onto the walls of the oven. After five more minutes, spray again, then bake for another 10 to 15 minutes until the bread is golden brown. The total baking time is 20 to 25 minutes. Leave to cool on a wire rack.

TIMELINE

· Make dough, prove for an hour
· Shape the loaf, prove for 30 minutes
· Score the top, rest for ten minutes
· Spray water in oven, bake loaf for five minutes
· Spray water in oven, bake for another five minutes
· Spray water in oven, bake for 10 to 15 minutes

Bits and Bobs

We always serve this relish with our venison burgers; it's also great with turkey and game during the festive season. For a quick and easy starter, stir a few spoonfuls through some sliced Brie and shredded chicken, wrap in filo pastry and oven bake till golden brown.

- Use fresh cranberries if they're in season – just add 60ml water to the recipe.

- If you don't have a muslin cloth, wrap the spices in a brand new J cloth instead. You need to be able to remove them before blitzing the sauce.

- Keep stirring as this cooks; the cranberries can be a pain and stick to the bottom of the pan. Serve at room temperature to get the best flavour.

- This keeps in the fridge for six months in an airtight jar.

Cranberry, Port and Orange Relish

Makes about 500ml

1 onion, finely diced
500g frozen cranberries
zest and juice of 1 orange
300ml port
300g granulated sugar
400ml red wine vinegar
1 teaspoon cloves
1 cinnamon stick, broken in half

muslin cloth for spices

Put the onion, cranberries, orange zest and juice, port, sugar and red wine vinegar in a large saucepan. Wrap the cloves and cinnamon stick in a piece of muslin and tie it up with string so none of the ingredients can escape, then add to the pan. Simmer, stirring, over a medium-low heat for 40 minutes until the relish has thickened to a jammy consistency. Discard the muslin parcel and pour the relish into a couple of clean jars (or a bowl if you're serving it immediately). Leave to cool.

Serve with warm crusty bread and slabs of strong, mature Cheddar = job done! This will take your ploughman's to a whole new level.

· If you're not into spicy food, leave out the chilli.

· The relish will thicken and set as it cools.

· This will keep for six months in an airtight container in the fridge.

Nippy Tomato, Apricot and Red Pepper Relish

Makes 1 litre

500g ripe tomatoes, cored and halved

2 medium white onions, halved and sliced

2 large red peppers, chopped into 3cm dice

1 medium red chilli, finely chopped (leave the seeds in if you like it hot)

850ml white wine vinegar

280g granulated sugar

190g whole dried apricots

3 tablespoons tomato purée

1 teaspoon paprika

1 teaspoon sea salt

Place your prepared tomatoes, onions, red peppers, chilli, vinegar, sugar and dried apricots in a large saucepan. Bring up to the boil over a medium-high heat, then turn down to a rolling simmer and cook for 70 minutes until all the ingredients are soft and the relish has thickened. Stir in the tomato purée, paprika and salt. Pour into a couple of clean jars or a heatproof, airtight container and leave to the side to cool. Pop in the fridge when it's cold.

This was how Nana got rid of the tomatoes that over-ran her glasshouse. There were only so many tomato sandwiches we could eat and nothing beats homemade tomato sauce. This one is tart and tangy – not at all like the usual sweet store-bought stuff. Serve with your barbecues or with anything wrapped in pastry and you are bound to impress!

· To make this gluten or wheat free, use red or white wine vinegar instead of malt.

· If you don't have a muslin cloth, wrap the spices in a brand new J cloth instead. You need to be able to remove them before blitzing the sauce.

· This is the only sauce for sausages straight off the barbecue and stuck between two slices of buttered white bread – it's awesome!

· Serve this with the Bacon and Egg Pie on page 131.

· You can store this in your cupboard or pantry, but once open, pop it in the fridge.

Homemade Tomato Sauce

Makes 1500ml

1kg ripe tomatoes,
   cored and halved
2 medium onions,
   roughly chopped
600ml malt vinegar
225g granulated sugar
200g sultanas
2 cooking apples,
   cored and roughly
   chopped with skin on
2 teaspoons paprika
1 teaspoon cayenne pepper
1 teaspoon ground allspice
1 tablespoon peppercorns
2 bay leaves
2 tablespoons tomato purée
1 teaspoon sea salt

muslin cloth for spices

Place your tomatoes, onions, vinegar, sugar, sultanas, apples, paprika, cayenne pepper and allspice into a large saucepan. Wrap the peppercorns and bay leaves in a piece of muslin and tie it up with a little bit of string so none of the ingredients can escape. Add it to the pan. Bring to the boil over a medium to high heat, then turn down to a rolling simmer.

Cook for an hour until the ingredients are soft and the sauce has thickened. Discard the muslin parcel, then blitz the sauce with a stick blender until smooth. Add your tomato purée and salt and blitz again to incorporate. You could now pass the sauce through a sieve to get a really smooth texture, but I prefer it with a little body. Pour into a couple of clean jars or bottles, seal and leave to cool.

We use this on our steak flatbreads. It is the perfect taste explosion for grilled meats, but is also incredible with grilled goats' cheese.

· This keeps in the fridge for ten days in an airtight jar.

Onion, Jalapeño and Raspberry Jam

Makes about 700ml

2 tablespoons olive oil

2 white onions,
  halved and thinly sliced

2 red onions,
  halved and thinly sliced

8 sprigs thyme, stalks removed,
  leaves chopped

110g granulated sugar

80ml balsamic vinegar

80ml red wine vinegar

125g frozen raspberries

2 tablespoons bottled jalapeños,
  drained and finely chopped

sea salt

cracked black pepper

Heat your olive oil in a heavy-bottomed saucepan over a medium heat. Fire in your sliced onions and thyme and sauté until the onions are soft and translucent. Sprinkle over the sugar and stir into the onions until it has dissolved. Add the balsamic and red wine vinegars and simmer for 20 minutes until you have a sticky, thick onion jam. There will still be a little juice in the pan – this is perfect. Add your raspberries and chopped jalapeños and stir for a couple of minutes until the raspberries have defrosted. Take off the heat and season to taste with salt and freshly cracked black pepper. Serve straight from the pan or pour into a clean airtight jar and pop into the fridge.

Nothing beats this with a plate of meats and cheeses; this is the cherry on the top for all antipastos or simply drizzled over your favourite meat.

· Spiced Apricot Sauce is just as good: just replace the plums with fresh apricots and swap the sultanas for dried apricots. I would also use 500ml white wine vinegar instead of red and white.

· If you don't have a muslin cloth, wrap the spices in a brand new J cloth instead. You need to be able to remove them before blitzing the sauce.

· You can store the sauce in an airtight jar in your cupboard or pantry but, once open, pop it in the fridge.

· This is awesome lightly warmed up with duck, pork or venison.

· A jar of this makes a really nice homemade Christmas gift, along with some quality local cheese. You will be sorted!

Spiced Plum Sauce

Makes 1 litre

400g ripe plums,
  stoned and halved
1 medium red onion,
  roughly chopped
250ml red wine vinegar
250ml white wine vinegar
130g dark brown sugar
50g sultanas
1 cooking apple, cored
  and roughly chopped
  with skin on
10g fresh ginger, peeled
  and finely chopped
½ teaspoon ground allspice
½ teaspoon peppercorns
1 cinnamon stick

muslin cloth for spices

Place your plums, onion, red and white wine vinegars, sugar, sultanas, apple, ginger and allspice into a large pan. Wrap the peppercorns and cinnamon stick in a piece of muslin and tie it up with some string so none of the ingredients can escape. Add to the pan.

Bring everything up to a boil over a medium-high heat, then turn down to a rolling simmer. Cook for an hour until the ingredients are soft and the sauce has thickened. Discard the muslin parcel, then blitz the sauce with a stick blender until smooth. Pour into a couple of clean jars or bottles, seal and leave to cool.

This recipe evolved because one of our chefs, Aggie, became obsessed with making the perfect eggs Benedict. It's perfect because it is minimal faff for maximum flavour and makes eggs and bacon into a great Sunday brunch. It's also a good way to use up any egg yolks left over from our Pavlova (page 209).

- If you don't have a food processor you can use a cake mixer with the balloon whisk or a hand-held electric mixer.

- Serve the hollandaise as soon as you can. If you must let it stand, leave it in a warm (not hot) place.

Hollandaise

Serves 4

125g butter, melted
3 large egg yolks
1 teaspoon wholegrain mustard
1 tablespoon lemon juice
1 tablespoon white wine vinegar
a pinch of salt
cracked black pepper

Put your melted butter in a jug. Put the egg yolks, mustard, lemon juice and white wine vinegar in the food processor bowl. Process for three to four minutes, until the yolks are pale, frothy and have roughly doubled in volume. With the motor still running, slowly drizzle the melted butter into the egg mix. Stop when you get to the milky solids at the bottom of the jug – don't add them. You will now have a frothy smooth sauce. Season with a little salt and black pepper and serve straight away.

Blinging Up Your Hummus

Here are a few combinations we use at the café... Just add the ingredients to the plain hummus recipe and blitz till smooth in the food processor.

Roasted Beetroot
120g roasted beetroot
1 teaspoon caraway seeds

Minted Pea
150g defrosted garden peas
15 mint leaves, finely chopped

Red Pepper and Chilli
2 red peppers,
   roasted with skin on
1 tablespoon sweet chilli sauce
1 teaspoon Tabasco

Sweet Potato and Paprika
120g roasted sweet potato
2 teaspoons paprika

An uber-fast starter, dip for veggie sticks or baguette-filler that tastes epic!

· Use the best quality tinned chickpeas you can get your hands on. You can cook your own, but we use tinned purely for convenience.

· This is a great way to get rid of leftover roast veggies! If you're roasting them specially, oil them very lightly with a little salt and pepper.

· Hummus keeps in the fridge, covered, for four days.

Hummus

Serves 4

1 x 400g tin chickpeas,
  drained and rinsed
125ml olive oil
3 tablespoons lemon juice
2 garlic cloves, finely chopped
2 tablespoons tahini
1½ teaspoons ground cumin
a small handful of
  coriander leaves
sea salt
cracked black pepper

Put your chickpeas, olive oil, lemon juice, garlic, tahini, cumin, and coriander in the food processor. Blitz until you have a really smooth paste. Taste and add salt and black pepper – you will need to season it really well, turning the mixer back on in between adding seasonings to make sure it's fully mixed.

I really love giant spoons of this with our Lamb Koftas (page 141) or Burgers (page 139), some roasted beetroot and warmed pitta breads. It is also perfect served with olives, roasted veg, hummus and breads as a grazing platter.

· Buy the best Greek yogurt you can get your hands on – 'Greek-style' yogurt is too runny.

· This keeps in the fridge for two days. Make sure you cover it, or it will taint everything else in the fridge.

· Don't chop your cucumber too fine or it will turn to mush.

Tzatziki

Serves 4

¼ cucumber
250g really good quality
  Greek yogurt
8 mint leaves, finely chopped
1 garlic clove, finely chopped
  or grated
1 teaspoon lemon zest
juice of 1 lemon
sea salt
cracked black pepper

To prepare the cucumber, cut it in half lengthwise and scrape out the seeds with a teaspoon. Slice the flesh into 1cm-thick crescents. Scrape your Greek yogurt into a mixing bowl and add the prepared cucumber, mint, garlic, lemon zest and juice. Mix together with a spoon and season with salt and black pepper to taste. You may want to add more mint or garlic – it's completely up to you.

Butter is my biggest weakness, especially when it's French! Here are a few combos that add a bang to a dish or mealtime.

· It's completely up to you whether you use salted or unsalted butter – just use whatever you prefer.

· These are just a few ideas – you can go wild with flavours, matching ingredients to your dishes.

· These will keep for seven days in the fridge, and you can also freeze them.

Butter with Bang

All the recipes make 125g

For whichever flavour you choose, combine all the ingredients in a wee bowl. Use a fork to mash everything together. Tip the butter out onto either clingfilm or greaseproof paper and roll into a tight sausage about 6cm in diameter. Twist the ends to seal and pop in the fridge or freezer until needed.

Paprika, Basil and Chilli

125g butter, softened
20 basil leaves, finely sliced
1 teaspoon ground paprika
1 small fresh chilli, deseeded
   and finely chopped
a grind of cracked black pepper

Suggestions for use:

· Melt over corn on the cob.
· Crush into boiled baby potatoes.
· Add to roasted sweet potato or butternut squash.
· Stir into mashed potatoes with some sliced spring onion.

Lemon, Garlic and Dill

125g butter, softened
1 small garlic clove,
   finely chopped or grated
4 sprigs dill, stalks removed,
   leaves finely chopped
zest of 1 lemon
a grind of cracked black pepper

Suggestions for use:

· Melt over barbecued mussels and prawns.
· Add a couple of knobs to the pan once you have pan-fried a bit of sole or white fish.
· Stuff under the breast skin when you roast a chicken – this adds flavour and gives you super-moist breast meat.

Thyme and Balsamic

125g butter, softened
8 sprigs thyme, stalks removed,
   leaves finely chopped
1 tablespoon balsamic glaze
a grind of cracked black pepper

Suggestions for use:

· Melt over steaks and chops.
· Serve with crusty hot breads.
· Put a knob in a freshly baked potato.

Great for garnishing foods, cooking, marinating or bread dipping.

· Pick a good quality, light olive oil that is not too intense in flavour.

· You mustn't boil the oil. You just want to gently warm it to take on the added flavours.

· I always strain the oil after it has infused; otherwise the flavouring ingredient can go mouldy or make the oil rancid.

· A sealed bottle will keep in a cool, dark place for up to six months.

Infused Oils

All the recipes makes 125ml

Place the oil and whatever flavouring you are using in a heavy-bottomed pan. On the lowest possible heat, gently warm the oil to the point when you can only just dip your finger in. It must not simmer or boil. Take off the heat, pour into a bowl or tub and leave to infuse at room temperature, covered, for 48 hours. Sieve into a bottle or jar. Keep in a cool, dark place. This will keep for six months.

Apple Oil

125ml olive oil
50g dried apple rings,
    chopped into small chunks

Suggestions for use:

· We drizzle this on our smoked fish soups.
· Great to bind a fresh salsa.

Rosemary Oil

125ml olive oil
6 sprigs rosemary

Suggestions for use:

· Toss parsnips and roast veggies in it before roasting.
· Use as your cooking oil for soups and stews.
· Serve with good bread as a dip.

Garlic Oil

125ml olive oil
3 garlic cloves, roughly chopped

Suggestions for use:

· Rub into steaks or chicken breasts before grilling.
· Use as your cooking oil for soups and stews.
· Serve with good bread as a dip.

A true taste of my childhood. Nana always had a jar of this in the fridge and chubby wee Kj would be forever spooning it into her belly! I use it now over muesli, in icings, drizzled over pavlova, in drinks and in salad dressings. It's so universal and gives a great tropical explosion to sweet and savoury dishes. Keep in the fridge for up to six months.

Passion Fruit Syrup

Makes 450ml

---

12 passion fruits
80ml water
225g granulated sugar

Cut the passion fruits in half and scrape out the pulp (including the seeds) with a teaspoon. Put the pulp into a small saucepan with the water and bring up to the boil over a high heat. Stir in the sugar and simmer for five minutes, until the sugar has dissolved and you have a bubbly, frothy sauce. Pour into a clean jam jar or tub and leave out to cool. Keep in the fridge.

A simple, tangy berry sauce. In the café we squiggle it on puddings, pancakes and yogurt. It also gives muesli a wee fruity punch.

· Use any berries you like – I like the tangy sweetness of raspberries.

· The coulis keeps for four days in the fridge.

Berry Coulis

Makes about 200ml

250g frozen raspberries
50ml lemon juice
70g caster sugar

On a low heat, gently simmer the berries, lemon juice and sugar until the berries are soft, the liquid has reduced by half and the sugar has dissolved. Blitz in a blender or with a stick blender until completely smooth, then pass through a fine sieve. Pour into a squeeze bottle or sauce jug and leave to cool.

Two of our team invented this one summer. Kev was our vegan chef and Meg worked out front. Meg has a whole list of awful food allergies, so they came up with this by chucking a bunch of things in the milkshake blender. I have to say, it's pretty damn good and it was awesome to see Meg enjoying a treat while the other staff munched on cakes and all the things she couldn't have. This is especially good if you have someone coming over for dinner who can't have dairy, wheat or gluten.

Tips from Kev and Meg, in their own words:

· You can make it with more than three bananas – freaky folks like us will have up to six. But for most people, three bananas make one serving. Freeze the bananas in bags, unpeeled and sliced.

· Avocado and cocoa nibs are other good freaky additions.

· Let the bananas soften out of the freezer for about ten minutes before you make this.

· This recipe is totally changeable – you can really add anything you want as long as you have the frozen bananas to make the bulk of your ice cream.

Kev and Meg's Freaky Vegan, Gluten Free Ice Cream

Serves 1–2

Kev's recipe:
3 frozen bananas
3 tablespoons peanut butter
2–3 tablespoons cocoa powder
maple or agave syrup to taste

Meg's recipe:
3 frozen bananas
130g frozen summer berries
a dash of vanilla extract
maple or agave syrup to taste

Chuck everything in a blender and blitz the hell out of it until you have a smooth, thick, ice-cream-y mass. Tip into a bowl and top with whatever goodies you want.

When I worked at Luca in London, this was the base for our Eton mess. You can eat it as it is or add lightly whipped cream and crumbled meringues and you have a five-minute pud that tastes the business.

- You can use any berries you like: I think raspberries, strawberries and brambles are a winner; red currants also give a nice burst too. Hull and half the strawberries first.

- Pleeeeeeeease make sure you use a really good quality balsamic vinegar – a nice sweet syrupy one – or your berries will taste nasty and vinegary. Otherwise use some lemon or orange juice instead!

- Serve the berries at room temperature to get the best of the flavours.

- This is brilliant spooned over sponge fingers. Let them soak into the fingers, then top with freshly whipped cream. Yum! If you really want to push the boat out, serve with homemade custard too.

Easy-peasy Balsamic Berry Pud

Serves 2 on its own or 4 with meringues and cream

400g fresh ripe berries
2 tablespoons icing sugar
½ teaspoon vanilla extract
  (or the pulp of a vanilla pod)
6 mint leaves, finely sliced
2 tablespoons really top-notch,
  syrupy balsamic vinegar

Place your berries in a mixing bowl and sprinkle in your icing sugar. Add the vanilla and the mint and drizzle over the balsamic. Using a rubber spatula, gently fold everything through until the berries are fully coated. Leave to marinate for about an hour before serving.

At the first café I worked at in New Zealand, we would make this sauce every day, just before service. It's delicious; it does test your patience with stirring-time, but it's well worth the wait! It's also a great way to get rid of any leftover egg yolks.

- No one wants scrambled egg custard so don't rush this by turning the hob up too high.

- If you have some vanilla sugar, use it for the sugar and you won't need the vanilla pod.

- If you're letting the custard stand in the pan before serving, put a layer of greaseproof paper directly onto the top of the custard – this will stop you getting a thick skin.

- The custard will keep in the fridge for two days, but you will struggle to reheat it without it splitting. So either eat it when you make it or have it cold.

- This is damn good in trifles and poured over hot rhubarb.

From-scratch Custard

(or, for you foodies, Crème Anglaise)

Serves 4

300ml double cream
1 small vanilla pod, scraped
3 large egg yolks
30g caster sugar

Put the cream and the pulp from the vanilla pod in a heavy-bottomed pan and warm over a medium heat to just before simmering point. Set aside. In a small metal bowl, whisk the yolks and sugar for four to five minutes, until the eggs become thicker and pale in colour. Pour the warm cream over the egg mixture in the bowl and give it a little whisk. Pour the mix back into the pan and put it over the lowest possible heat. Stand and patiently stir the sauce with a wooden spoon until it starts to thicken – about eight to ten minutes. When it's ready, it will coat the back of the wooden spoon and if you run your finger across it the line will stay. Don't whisk the custard as it will make it frothy and can taint the flavour and colour.

We use a huge amount of vanilla pods at the café. They are insanely expensive so we never bin the empty pods – we infuse caster sugar with them and use it in our baking and to poach fruit. Here's how to get more bang from your buck!

· Make sure the jar or container you are keeping your sugar in is dry and airtight so no moisture gets in.

· Use vanilla sugar in your baking and you won't need to use any vanilla extract. It's great in whipped cream too.

· You can adapt this recipe to make lavender sugar by using 1 teaspoon dried lavender per 150g sugar. It makes delicious shortbread.

Vanilla Sugar

Makes 500g

500g caster sugar
4 or 5 empty vanilla pods

Put your sugar in a large, dry, airtight jar. Whenever you have an empty vanilla pod, bury it in the sugar and leave to infuse. I would leave it for a minimum of a week. When you want to use it, pop the sugar and pods straight into a food processor and blitz till the pods are broken down and dispersed through the sugar. Sieve and discard any stray lumps of vanilla pod. Return the sugar to the airtight jar to store.

Drinks

Smoothies and Shakes

Mountain Cafe smoothies and shakes have been curing hangovers, quenching giant thirsts and satisfying folks for years now. Not to mention tipping our front of house team over the edge on busy summer days, especially when the chefs want them too!

Berry Smoothie

Serves 1

240g frozen fruits of
 the forest berries
100ml cranberry juice
100ml apple juice

Place everything into a blender and blitz until thick and smooth.

Banana Smoothie

Serves 1

Whenever we have bananas starting to over-ripen, we simply chop them up and freeze them for our smoothies. It is a great way to thicken and chill your smoothies down and to stop banana waste.

---

1 frozen chopped banana
100g Greek-style yogurt
80ml full fat milk
a pinch of cinnamon
a pinch of nutmeg
1 scoop vanilla ice cream

Put everything into a blender and blitz until thick and smooth

Struggle for time in the mornings for a healthy breakfast? This is the perfect sip-on-the-way-to-work boost everyone needs. It's my life's-a-bit-mental breakfast. I used to start my day with flat whites and no breakfast until I created this and it helped me lose weight and have more energy without having to sit down and eat.

- If you don't have fresh fruit or fruit salad to hand, get some tinned fruit in juice. Or just chuck in something from the fruit bowl.

- Instead of dairy milk, you can use soya, rice or almond milk or fruit juice.

- For a gluten free version, replace the granola with some dried cranberries, desiccated coconut and flaked almonds.

- The granola does make it a bit hard to use a straw, so you may have to contend with having a smoothie moustache.

Breakfast Smoothie

Makes 1 huge or 2 small glasses

---

1 banana
100ml milk
200g fresh fruit salad
  or tinned fruit
130g fresh or frozen berries
50g granola
1 tablespoon honey

Place everything in a blender and blitz until thick.

Coffee Shake

Serves 1

**We use espresso for this, but strong stove-top or instant coffee
will be just as good.**

50ml strong coffee

4 scoops vanilla ice cream

100ml full fat milk

Place everything into a blender and blitz until thick
and smooth

Iced Chocolate

Serves 1

---

chocolate ice cream sauce

3 scoops vanilla ice cream

250ml full fat milk

4 teaspoons chocolate
milkshake powder

Drizzle some chocolate sauce around the inside of the glass.
Scoop the ice cream into the glass. In a blender, blitz the milk
and milkshake powder. Pour slowly over the ice cream and
serve with a straw and a spoon, unless you want a big mess.

Having a cocktail party? This needs to be on the list! With or without added booze it looks really classy and tastes berry-licious.

- If it's blaeberry season, pick your own. Just wash and crush them a little before putting them in the pan.

- Make sure the blueberry liquid is cold when you put it in the blender, or you have a good chance of blowing the lid off and wearing it. Trust me, I have done it!

- This will keep in the fridge for a month in an airtight bottle.

- If I was adding booze, I would slosh in some vodka or gin with a bit of fresh mint.

Blueberry Fizz

Makes 800ml concentrated juice

500ml water
400g sugar
320g frozen blueberries
70ml lemon juice
sparkling water to serve

Put the water, sugar and frozen blueberries into a heavy-bottomed pan. Bring up to the boil over a medium-high heat, then take off the heat. Add the lemon juice and leave to let the flavours infuse as it cools.

When it's cold, blitz in a food processor or with a stick blender until liquidised. Sieve the liquid into a bowl or tub, taste and add some more lemon juice if you like your juice a little tart. Remember that this is the concentrate so it will seem very sweet and strong. Put the bowl in the fridge – as it chills, foam will set on the top so gently scrape this off.

Pour the cordial into a bottle or jar and keep in the fridge. To serve, pour the desired amount of cordial over ice into a glass or jug and top up with sparkling water (and booze). I like it with half cordial and half sparkling water.

Perfect party juice, a great hot-day sipper and a must at barbecues.

· This will keep for seven days in an airtight bottle in the fridge.

· To make fizzy lemonade, fill your glass three-quarters full and top up with sparkling water.

· You can use any berries or fruit you like here: rhubarb is delicious, and gooseberry and elderflower work really well.

· Freeze into ice cube trays and add a few cubes to a vodka and soda. Warning: you may lose use of your legs, like I did.

Bramble Lemonade

Makes 850ml

150g caster sugar
100g frozen brambles
650ml cold water
200ml fresh lemon juice
5 mint leaves, roughly chopped

Bring the sugar, brambles and 200ml of the water to boil in a saucepan. Take off the heat when it starts boiling and the sugar has dissolved. Add the lemon juice, the remaining 450ml water and the mint and stir. Leave to infuse in the fridge for at least an hour, then sieve and pour into an airtight bottle. Keep it in the fridge until you want to drink it, then serve over ice with some chopped mint and frozen lemon slices.

Nothing beats the sweetness of a ripe pineapple. This is the perfect drink to go with a lazy weekend brunch.

· You will find that a thick foam naturally forms on the top of the juice – this is just the proteins reacting to being in the blender. Either scrape it off or drink it like a pineapple-cino.

· This is awesome with a dash of Malibu over ice.

· Instead of throwing the pineapple pulp away, try it in scones with a little coconut and some chopped white chocolate.

· This will keep for five days in an airtight bottle in the fridge.

Pineapple and Mint Juice

Makes about 750ml

1 small, ripe pineapple
400ml pineapple juice
8–12 mint leaves, finely sliced

Peel and core the pineapple, then cut into thin slices. Place in a food processor or a smoothie machine with a dash of the pineapple juice and blitz until completely smooth. Add the rest of the juice and sieve into a large bowl. Stir together until well mixed and discard whatever's left in the sieve. Add your mint and refrigerate for at least an hour. The juice will naturally separate so give it a stir before serving over ice. Garnish with some mint tips.

This juice started as a chilled summer soup which freaked folks out, so then it evolved into a juice. It is one of the most refreshing drinks on a hot summer's day.

· I use a good quality cloudy apple juice as it's less sweet.

· If you can only get a large melon, pour the juice into ice cube trays to make watermelon iced-lollies for the kids.

Watermelon and Basil Juice

Makes about 2 litres (depending on size of melon)

1 small watermelon
400ml good quality
   cloudy apple juice
5 leaves basil, finely sliced

Peel the melon and chop it, seeds and all, into medium-sized chunks. Put in a food processor or a smoothie machine with a dash of apple juice and blitz until completely smooth. Sieve into a large bowl and discard the pulp left in the sieve. Add the remaining apple juice and your basil, stir and refrigerate for at least an hour before drinking.

It will have separated, so give it a stir before serving it over ice. Garnish with some ripped basil leaves.

Mulled drinks

Every winter I love to look out of the kitchen at around 4pm to see the café full of skiers, walkers, climbers and winter adventurers, sipping our hot drink specials and devouring cakes after an epic day in the Cairngorms.

Non-alcoholic Mulled Apple and Pomegranate Juice

Makes about 1 litre

700ml cloudy apple juice
300ml pomegranate juice
2 tablespoons vanilla sugar
1 pomegranate, seeds only
8 allspice berries
4 whole cloves
2 cinnamon sticks

Place everything in a heavy-bottomed pan and bring to a rolling boil for ten minutes. Reduce to a simmer for another ten minutes. Taste and add extra pomegranate juice or sugar as you like.

Mulled Cider

Makes about 1 litre

500ml cider
300ml cloudy apple juice
200ml ginger ale
70ml spiced rum
2 tablespoons honey
6 whole cloves
2 cinnamon sticks

Place everything in a heavy-bottomed pan and bring to a rolling boil for five to ten minutes. Reduce to a simmer for another 15 minutes. Taste and add extra apple juice, rum or honey if needed. Serve with some thin slices of Granny Smith apples for a bit of bite.

Jamaican Rum Punch

Makes about 800ml

350ml dark rum
300ml apple cider
200ml cloudy apple juice
1 vanilla pod, scraped
6 star anise
2 cinnamon sticks
6 whole cloves
4 tablespoons honey
50ml lemon juice

Place everything (including the vanilla pulp and pod) in a heavy-bottomed pan and bring to a rolling boil for five to ten minutes. Reduce to a simmer for another 15 minutes. Taste and add extra rum, apple juice or honey as you like.

Mulled wine

Makes about 1 litre

750ml red wine (not super
    expensive, just a decent drop)
100ml orange juice
100ml diluting Ribena
70ml brandy
100g vanilla sugar
2 whole cloves
2 star anise
1 cinnamon stick
2 cardamom pods

Place everything in a heavy-bottomed pan and bring to the boil for 10 to 15 minutes. Reduce to a simmer for 30 minutes to an hour. Taste and add extra brandy, sugar or orange juice as you like.

Chocolate, a wee kick of chilli and the warmth of spices, sitting in front of the fire after being out in winter: it's a winning combination and the best way to finish a day.

- If you only have unsweetened cocoa powder, add sugar to taste.

- We make up our hot chocolate powder in bulk and keep it in a jar at the café. Just scale up the dry ingredients if you want to do the same.

- If you happen to have a coffee machine with a milk wand at home, then make this by the mug. Put two tablespoons of the spiced hot chocolate powder into a mug and add a little boiling water to make a smooth slurry. Steam enough milk to fill the mug, and pour it over the chocolate mix. That's how we do it.

- Don't boil your milk; you just want to bring it up to drinking temperature. If you scald it you kill the natural sugars in the milk, making a bitter drink that also burns your mouth!

Spiced Hot Chocolate

Serves 4

8 tablespoons hot chocolate
  (we use 50% sweetened cocoa)
1½ teaspoons ground cinnamon
1½ teaspoons ground cardamom
1 teaspoon mild chilli powder
1 litre full fat milk

Warm the milk in a heavy-bottomed pan over a medium-low heat. When it's at drinking temperature, sprinkle in the hot chocolate powder, cinnamon, cardamom and chilli powder. Whisk in really well, pour into cups and serve straight away.

There is No 'I' in Team

The hardest part of any business is running a team of staff smoothly and efficiently, especially in hospitality. I have always been incredibly lucky with our team members, folks that have committed their time, sweat and tears to help me to get the café to where it is today. Nothing makes me happier or more proud than when I look out of the pass and it's crazy busy, but the team are happy with everything running 100%.

A huge thanks to all our team, past and present. Special kitchen wall of fame mention goes out to John Coghill for helping me see potential in myself and others; Tony Cumming for banter, banter and more banter; Adam Anderson for his karaoke clean downs and the best fish cakes on the planet; Agata Galicka for systems, systems, systems and for being my right hand lady and good friend for six years; Kevin Riddoch for being a big vegan hippy chef with awesome baking and mountain biking skills; Laura Cantwell for being a total grafter who keeps me sane when the going gets tough and Sam Hawkins for his all-day-breakfast stacking challenges and being our kitchen version of Tigger. Front of house, I have to give a shout out to Claire Smith, our fantastic manager who runs front of house, 12 staff and a family of five – she is an absolute legend and lifesaver; Emily Haggerty who started as a dishwasher when she was 13 and stayed with us for seven years to become the best barista we have ever had; Rachel Williams for her procedures, organisation and signs; Keely Foley, my front of house guru and rock in the early days who totally got what I was trying to do; Belinda Althaus, a wee Aussie rocket who had more enthusiasm and energy than the whole team put together; Fiona Quire who is just a completely mental local lassie who will always be part of the MC family; Sue Williams, my first ever employee, so friendly, great with customers and a true friend who also tested a lot of the recipes in the book; Elizabeth Pirie (Squizz), our wee in-house artist and clean freak who was obsessed with cleaning the cake fridge and keeping everything tidy and who did the awesome illustrations for this book; Kate Streib, a lovely Canadian lass and environment freak who helped set up all our environmental policies; Marius Swart, a South African bloke who was a hard worker and party animal with incredible banter – he made me laugh every day; and finally Courtney Saunders, a sweet little South African girl who was everything you could ask for in a server – she was so kind to customers and nothing was ever an issue.

A special thanks goes to finance guru Andy and my Rottweiler bookkeeper Lisa, who breathed reality into a crazy café and a stubborn Kiwi chef. You guys drive me mad, but the café wouldn't be here without you!

A huge thank you to my incredible parents-in-law, Ann and Andrew. They have always backed me up and lent me huge amounts of money, even though I had only been married to their son for 18 months! You guys are the best parents-in-law a girl could ever ask for. A humble thank you goes to my husband Al. He has not only put up with my non-stop drive and endless long shifts but has actually supported me and pushed me to follow all my dreams. He has inspired me to occasionally step away from the café and visit amazing wild places around Scotland by bike, boat and foot.

Finally, if it hadn't been for my maternal grandparents and finding a career in cheffing I'm not sure where I would be now. I am forever indebted to them for never giving up on me, even when I was a total nightmare, going off the rails and pushing every boundary going. They always reined me back in and showered me with love. Life was always an adventure and an education with Granddad and Nana. I dedicate this book to them.

Index